# Aid for Peace

The publication of this book has been supported by

commissioned by

gtz | Crisis Prevention and Conflict Transformation

Federal Ministry
for Economic Cooperation
and Development

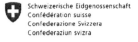

Schweizerische Eidgenossenschaft
Confédération suisse
Confederazione Svizzera
Confederaziun svizra

Direktion für Entwicklung und Zusammenarbeit DEZA
Direction du développement et de la coopération DDC
Swiss Agency for Development and Cooperation SDC
Agencia Suiza para el desarrollo y la cooperación COSUDE

Austrian
Development Cooperation

Belgian
Development Cooperation
.be

Thania Paffenholz | Luc Reychler

# Aid for Peace

## A Guide to Planning and Evaluation for Conflict Zones

 Nomos

Frontispiece:
© Manoocher Deghati/IRIN

Die Deutsche Nationalbibliothek lists this publication in the
Deutsche Nationalbibliografie; detailed bibliographic data is available
in the Internet at http://www.d-nb.de .

ISBN 978-3-8329-2582-6

1. Edition 2007

# Contents

# List of Figures

# Preface

Two-thirds of the countries in the world today are either suffering from political tensions and armed conflict or else they find themselves in the aftermath of a destructive conflict or war. As a consequence, local and international organizations are working in these zones of armed conflict to reduce the suffering of the population by helping to reinstall security, monitor human rights, build peace or by supporting efforts to rebuild the democratic and economic structures that are essential for maintaining a lasting peace.

The 'Aid for Peace' approach was developed in an attempt to satisfy a set of interrelated needs in the fields of peacebuilding, development and humanitarian action:

First, it answers to the demand for more systematic reflection on the individual and collective assumptions that guide the planning and evaluation of interventions in conflict zones. Policy-makers, practitioners, researchers and educators working in these conflict zones should be encouraged to critically reflect on their normative, theoretical and epistemological stances.

Second, the approach provides a standard methodology for planning and evaluating peacebuilding interventions such as negotiations, reconciliation, civil society or other peace initiatives. 'Aid for Peace' thereby merges these procedures with the core values and objectives of peacebuilding: a vision for peacebuilding and hypotheses of change to contribute to conflict transformation and social change that also allow peacebuilding actors to know how their intervention fits into the multi-sector, multi-level tapestry of peacebuilding.

Third, 'Aid for Peace' responds to the need to integrate the 'conflict and peace lens' into standard operational planning and evaluation procedures of development and humanitarian interventions. Almost all donor and implementing organizations now have a strategy for conflict sensitive development and/or a staff position or unit dedicated to issues of conflict and peace.

Fourth, 'Aid for Peace' wants to support actors to recognize the political dimension of peacebuilding, development and humanitarian action. Conflict settings are highly political and characterized by uncertainty, unpredictability, competing values and interests, and a struggle for power. Aid and peace work in such settings requires not only analytic skills, but also imagination, creativity, political savvy, careful consideration of the use and available forms of power, and a great deal of courage. The 'Aid for Peace' framework is designed to help make those consequences more explicit so that actors can make informed, conflict-sensitive, peace-enhancing decisions and strategies.

Finally, 'Aid for Peace' helps to reflect the macro-level 'big' picture of peacebuilding. The focus on the big picture also reflects the peacebuilding process as a whole and deals with the interdependence of different peacebuilding interventions, tries to anticipate cross effects and reminds us that peacebuilding is a complex process involving multiple transformations at the same time.

The 'Aid for Peace' approach builds on a wealth of different research and practitioner experiences from the peace, development and humanitarian, as well as, the evaluation field. In this way it wants to contribute to the further development of the two important debates about a) linking conflict, peace and development; and b) professionalization in peacebuilding.

The development of the 'Aid for Peace' approach started in 1996 under the label of 'Conflict Impact Assessment Systems' (CIAS) with the primary objective of providing an assessment framework for macro level policy interventions related to conflicts and peace processes (Reychler 1999b).

The movement from CIAS to the comprehensive 'Aid for Peace' approach has been largely influenced by the different debates about 'Peace and Conflict Impact Assessment' (PCIA) (Bush 1998), 'Do no Harm' (Anderson 1999) as well as 'conflict sensitive development approaches (Nyheim / Gaigals / Leonhardt 2001; De la Haye / Denayer 2003, Bush 2003 and Paffenholz 2005d) but also by the more recent debate about evaluation in peacebuilding (Church / Shouldice 2002; Smith 2003; Anderson / Olson 2003; Paffenholz 2005a; Fast / Neufeld 2005 and Church / Rogers 2006).

From 2000 onwards a framework had been developed that combined assessment of macro political conflicts and peace processes with assessment of development and humanitarian programs in conflict zones in terms of their peace and conflict sensitivity. This research involved on-going field testing in different countries in cooperation with donors and agencies. The researchers who conducted the studies assessed, evaluated, or supported peace and conflict sensitive planning processes at the invitation of donors and agencies. Consequently, the authors jointly developed the CIAS into the 'Aid for Peace' framework while Thania Paffenholz additionally developed the different practical application forms of the framework as presented in parts II and III of the book.

The objective of this book is therefore to provide a practical guide to planning and evaluation for and in conflict zones as an attempt to share our research and practical experiences over the last years and help further pursue the respective research and practitioner debates. Thus, this book does not provide a theoretical background for peacebuilding as this has been done by many other publications including our own 'Peacebuilding' book (Reychler / Paffenholz 2001).

*Defining our terms*

When we talk about conflict in this book, we focus on destructive forms of armed conflict or war. This is also valid when we mention the term 'conflict zones' which always implies zones of 'armed conflict'.

Peacebuilding is understood as an overarching term to describe a long-term process covering all activities that aim at preventing and managing armed conflict and sustaining peace after large-scale organized violence has ended. Peacebuilding covers all activities that are linked directly to this objective over five to ten years. It should create conducive conditions for economic reconstruction, development and democratization, but should not be equated and thus confused with these concepts.

When we talk about *'peacebuilding interventions'* in this book, we therefore look at the objective of the intervention and focus on those interventions that aim to *directly* contribute to peacebuilding (as defined above) in a country or area and have peacebuilding as a primary objective. These types of interventions can be on the policy level (such as official or unofficial mediation or facilitation efforts or official post-conflict efforts such as Truth Commissions), or on the program or project level (such as disarmament, demobilization or reintegration of ex-combatants, negotiation or conflict resolution training, peace education, empowerment of civil society peace groups or activities to deal with the destroyed relationships of people after armed conflicts such as reconciliation or dialogue projects).

When we talk about *development, humanitarian, or sometimes just 'aid' interventions*, we mean all other interventions that have primary objectives other than peacebuilding but that take place in areas affected by armed conflict or in the aftermath of a war. The primary objective of these interventions is to contribute to the development of a country or region or to reduce human suffering. Here we include development policy or program / project interventions in different sectors such as water, health, or agriculture and humanitarian work. When these interventions take place in conflict zones they need to a) reduce the conflict-related risks, b) ensure that they will not have unintended negative effects on conflict dynamics and c) assess if the intervention can *indirectly* contribute to peacebuilding through their development or humanitarian activities. When we talk about 'peace and conflict sensitivity' in this book we refer to this indirect contribution of development and humanitarian actors to reducing negative effects of their work on conflict and enhancing positive effects on peacebuilding.

In case development or humanitarian actors want to *directly* contribute to peacebuilding with interventions having peacebuilding as a primary objective, we treat them as direct peacebuilding interventions as described above.

Throughout this book, we use the term *'project'* to refer to a group of activities designed to advance a specific purpose in a fixed time frame and *'program'* to refer to a series of coordinated projects. When we talk about 'programs' we refer to both programs and projects. We use the term *'policy'* to discuss macro interventions for both peacebuilding and development of a country or region. Macro-level peacebuilding policy intervention can, for example, be diplomatic support for national mediation or facilitation efforts, while macro-level development policy interventions could include budgetary support to a national government. A development country program usually comprises both program- and policy-oriented interventions.

## Structure of the book

The book is structured in four parts: Part I provides a basic introduction to the 'Aid for Peace' approach, part II focuses on peacebuilding interventions, part III on development and humanitarian interventions and part IV gives answers to frequently asked questions. Part I thereby provides an overview of the 'Aid for Peace' core concept and methodological framework while parts II and III walk the user through the application process and part IV provides the user with detailed practical tools.

# Acknowledgments

We want to thank the many people and organizations who have supported our efforts in writing this book. First, we thank the Belgian Department of International Cooperation for financially supporting the development of the 'Aid for Peace' approach as well as the German Technical Cooperation Agency, the German Ministry of Economic Cooperation and Development, the Swiss Agency for Development and Cooperation and the Austrian Development Agency for their financial support to the publishing of the book.

We especially thank Christoph Spurk for his continuous critical reflections on the development of the approach, his excellent comments on different versions of the manuscript, and his moral support throughout the entire project.

We also thank all other people who helped in the conceptual development of the 'Aid for Peace' approach through sharing critical reflections and comments: Louis Kriesberg, Cornelia Brinkmann, Ulrike Hopp, Markus Meier, Nathan Horst, Mohammed Abu-Nimer, Erin McCandless, Markus Heininger, Jörg Frieden, Günther Bächler, Thierry Regnass, Riccardo Bocco and Magdalena Bernath. Special thanks go to the people who have given substantial comments on parts of the manuscript: Ulrike Hopp, Kai Leonhardt, Michaela Zintl and Susanna Campbell. Many thanks also to Maia Carter Hallward for her comments and an extraordinary job of proof-reading and editing.

We also wish to extend thanks to the Berghof Handbook team for providing an excellent discussion forum on our approach in their online PCIA dialogue series (www.berghof-handbook.net/pcia_newtrends.htm): Thanks for good discussion to Oliver Wils, Beatrix Schmelzle, Martina Fischer, David Bloomfield and the other discussants Kenneth Bush, Adam Barbolet, Rachel Goldwyn, Hesta Groenewald and Andrew Sherriff.

We are grateful to the German Technical Cooperation Agency (GTZ) for its collaboration in general, as well as for its help with field testing and training, including the many useful discussions we had with many of the GTZ staff. We owe a special word of gratitude to Uwe Kievelitz, Dunja Brede, Gabriele Kruk, Roland Steurer, Christoph Feyen, Johannes Knapp, Ramesh Shestra, Sonja Vorwerk, Mareike Jung, Sabine Becker and Kai Leonhardt. Thanks also to Marei John, Nele Förch, Almut Wieland-Karimi, and Anja Dargatz of the Friedrich-Ebert-Stiftung for their cooperation on results chains, to Hilde Van den Bulck and Christoph Spurk for their cooperation on media, to Anna-Karen Regenass for her information on scenario building, to the International Labour Organization (ILO), the Swiss Development Cooperation (SDC), the International Bureau of Education/UNESCO, the Life and Peace Institute (LPI), the Swedish Development Cooperation (SIDA), the European Commission, the United Nation Development Program (UNDP) and the Belgian

Development Cooperation for their support in the field testing for the approach and to the many organizations that invited us to present and discuss the 'Aid for Peace' approach at various occasions.

Thanks also to the active members of the assessment teams who supported our work during the early field phase – Stefaan Calmeyn, Tatian Musabyimana, Eveline Rooijmans, Ilse De Vlieger, Jos de la Haye, Jeroen Seynhaeve, Koenraad Denayer, and Eva Smets – and to the participants in the training courses that were held during 2003 and 2004. The many discussions we held with these individuals helped us tremendously in the further development of the approach. Special thanks go to the participants in the training course held in Berne in April 2004.

Thank you to Sheila Reed for providing an excellent training course on humanitarian evaluations, which provoked a great deal of fruitful reflection on the link between the 'Aid for Peace' approach and evaluations.

Thank you also to Lynne Rienner for many helpful discussions on the structure of the book.

A word of appreciation also goes to the staff of the Field Diplomacy Initiative (Leuven) and the Center for Peace Research and Strategic Studies at the University of Leuven, Belgium. Special thanks go also to a number of people who have supported the process of final editing and/or publication of the book: Richard Lappin, Daniel Paffenholz, Gabrielle Kruk, Christian Strehlein, Susanne Schreiber, Beate Bernstein and Cristina Hoyos.

# Part I

# Introducing the 'Aid for Peace' Approach

# 1 Understanding the Background and Objectives

Armed conflicts have become one of the major concerns in foreign policy as well as in development cooperation and humanitarian action.

Over the past couple of years researchers and practitioners have been developing policy instruments, operational approaches and tools for better work in and for conflict zones. The development and humanitarian community has become aware of the need to 'Do no Harm' (by seeking to avoid unintended negative effects of aid interventions on conflict dynamics and support local capacities for peace (Anderson 1999). The peacebuilding community has started looking into ways and means of more effectively contributing to peacebuilding through evaluating and professionalizing peacebuilding efforts.

To date, however, no comprehensive framework has been developed to systematically plan and evaluate – and thus improve – both development and peacebuilding interventions. Although both communities have drawn lessons from each other, much institutionalization remains to be done, on the policy as well as on the program and project level. All existing approaches so far focus on either type of intervention (development or peacebuilding) or are limited to a certain level of intervention (policy, program or project). We developed the 'Aid for Peace' approach in an effort to fill this gap and thereby contribute to the further development of the international debates on:

- linking development, humanitarian action and peacebuilding, e.g. making development and humanitarian interventions more sensitive towards conflict dynamics and also support them in contributing directly or indirectly to peacebuilding;
- enhancing the effectiveness and the impact of peacebuilding work by a) introducing planning and evaluation procedures and b) working to alleviate the false assumption that the move towards more professionalization and improved monitoring and evaluation processes in the field of peacebuilding is a donor-driven idea that unnecessarily complicates peacebuilding work. Instead, we argue that this emphasis is a logical consequence of the rapid and intense evolution of the conflict resolution/peacebuilding field during the last decade;
- emphasizing the operational as well as the policy level of interventions in conflict zones in order to underline that peacebuilding and conflict are political issues and that policy interventions, just like project or program interventions, need to be planned, monitored, and evaluated systematically in order to be effective.

# 2   What is the 'Aid for Peace' Approach all about?

The 'Aid for Peace' Approach seeks to facilitate the planning and evaluation of peacebuilding, development and humanitarian interventions and to provide a systematic approach that links analysis with implementation. It is particularly designed for interventions taking place in situations of latent or manifest armed conflict or in the aftermath of armed conflict or war.

The 'Aid for Peace' approach can be used by actors in a variety of sectors (public, private, non-governmental), on different levels (local, national, international), and by those involved in all the various stages of interventions in conflict zone, from policy makers to donors to those implementing peace, development, or humanitarian interventions.

The 'Aid for Peace' framework provides a common methodological framework for planning and evaluating peacebuilding and development or humanitarian policy and program interventions.

The purpose of applying 'Aid for Peace' to peacebuilding interventions (part II) is: a) to ensure the peacebuilding relevance of the intervention, b) to improve the effects of the intervention on peacebuilding (in terms of outcomes and impact), c) to avoid unintended conflict risks and d) to contribute to the development of systematic planning, monitoring and evaluation procedures for peacebuilding interventions.

In contrast with peacebuilding interventions, the primary goal of development and humanitarian interventions is to contribute to the economic and social development of a country or region or to reduce human suffering. The purpose of applying the 'Aid for Peace' approach in development and humanitarian work (part III ) is to a) ensure that the intervention will not have unintended negative effects on conflict dynamics, b) reduce the risks the intervention might encounter in areas of armed conflict, c) assess if the intervention can also have positive effects on peacebuilding in addition to the development goal and d) embed considerations of peace and conflict dynamics into standard development and humanitarian planning, monitoring and evaluation procedures comparable to the gender or environmental lens.

# 3   The 'Aid for Peace' Framework and its Applications

The 'Aid for Peace' framework forms the basis for planning, assessing or evaluating peacebuilding, development or humanitarian interventions. However, its application differs for the various types of interventions (peacebuilding, development or humanitarian) and for what purpose it is used (planning, assessment or evaluation).

The general framework consists of four parts (see Figure 1):
1) An analysis of the peacebuilding needs in a given country, area or region,
2) An assessment of the peacebuilding relevance of the planned or existing intervention,
3) An assessment of the conflict risks (expected or manifest effects of the conflict on the intervention activities), and
4) An assessment of the expected or manifest effects of the intervention on the conflict dynamics and the peacebuilding process (peace and conflict outcomes and impact).

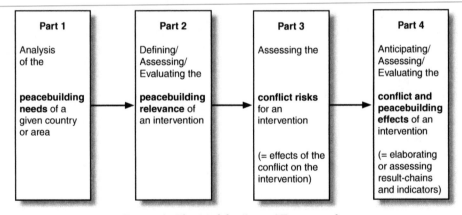

*Figure 1: The 'Aid for Peace' Framework.*

## Analyzing the Peacebuilding Needs: Part 1

The analysis of the peacebuilding needs in a particular country or area provides the foundation for subsequent parts of the analytical framework. The peacebuilding needs are assessed in four consecutive steps:
1) Analyzing the conflict and peace environment;
2) Anticipating conflict dynamics and peacebuilding;
3) Analyzing peacebuilding deficiencies: Eliciting the peacebuilding vision

of stakeholders in order to make current deficiencies – as well as the desired outcomes – clear and transparent;

4) Specifying the needs for peacebuilding in the respective country, region or area and/or in a particular development sector.

*Step 1: Analyzing the conflict and peacebuilding environment*

The objective in the first step of the peacebuilding needs assessment involves analyzing both the conflict dynamics and the peacebuilding process of a country or area. The analysis can be made at the macro-, sector- or micro level and focuses on what has happened as well as what is currently happening. For interventions at the country program or policy level, we analyze the causes and dynamics of conflict and the peacebuilding process at the macro level. When applying the framework on the program level, we briefly analyze the overall conflict and peace situation of a country, but focus mainly on the conflict and peacebuilding situation in the geographical area of intervention. For programs or projects that address a particular development sector, we need to add an analysis of the specific conflicts and peace-related factors relevant for that sector. Information about the general needs in a particular development sector is usually available in the form of donor, agency or governmental needs assessments. In order to find out which issues in this sectoral analysis are relevant, the sectoral assessments need to be compared with the conflict/ peacebuilding analysis.

To give an example of how this process occurs, we will walk you through the stages of an assessment we conducted in Sri Lanka of a development program focusing on employment creation by supporting small and medium sized enterprise (SME) development. When we conducted the peace and conflict assessment, the program had not yet started, but the initial program planning had been finalized and the countrywide needs assessment in the sector, as well as a more specific assessment for the geographical program area, was already available. In addition to these existing assessments, we conducted a macro-level conflict and peace analysis of the situation in Sri Lanka, followed by an analysis of the conflicts, tensions and peacebuilding potential in those districts where the program was to be implemented. The latter study included re-examining the findings of the existing sectoral needs analysis using a conflict/peace lens. Local research teams took primary responsibility for carrying out the two studies. We then made use of the results to guide further field assessment. The results of both field assessments were then discussed with involved stakeholders in a participatory workshop (see more details in chapter 8).

There are many methods available for analyzing the conflict dynamics and peacebuilding processes. Regardless of the chosen method, some essential variables must be analyzed: parties involved in the conflict, issues at stake, root causes of the conflict, conflict escalating and de-escalating factors. In this step we also need to integrate a gender lens to explore how men and women are affected by conflict differently (see more information in chapter 12).

18

*Step 2: Anticipating conflict dynamics and peacebuilding*

As the situation in a conflict zone is subject to rapid change, peacebuilding and development actors must anticipate possible developments in the conflict dynamics and the peacebuilding process. Understanding and envisioning different possible future scenarios helps intervening actors be more flexible in adapting their interventions as new situations arises. Advance thinking also enhances the capacity of such actors to react more systematically to changed contexts.

A good conflict and peacebuilding analysis paves the way for anticipating possible future developments both in terms of conflict dynamics and the peacebuilding process. There are a number of methods and tools that can be used for anticipating future developments, most of which are carried out in partnership with local stakeholders or involve interviews with a representative set of key actors. One useful way of approaching the future is to consider the probability of different future scenarios (Schwartz 1991, Wack 1985) and identify the factors which influence the conflict and peace dynamics leading to such scenarios. Another method involves identifying the main conflict escalating and de-escalating factors and conducting a comparative analysis of relative strength. When conflict escalating forces are stronger than the conflict de-escalating forces, we can expect the conflict to continue and possibly escalate, and vice versa.

In the example of the Sri Lankan SME program, we developed different scenarios for the near future in order to prepare the program for possible future developments (e.g. the peace process improves and leads to a more suitable business environment) and a worst-case scenario (e.g. violence escalates in program area). Such future contingency plans may arise organically from the first step of this process, which assesses the conflict and peace environment. At this step, however, discussions should focus on better understanding the risks and opportunities within each of the different future scenarios.

*Step 3: Identifying the peacebuilding deficiencies: clarifying stakeholders' visions for peacebuilding*

To identify the peacebuilding deficiencies that prevail one has to

a) define the peace one wants to achieve (i.e. explain or develop a vision for peacebuilding),
b) specify the conditions that would enhance the peacebuilding process, and
c) compare the present with the envisaged situation of peace.

Without clearly and transparently defining a vision of the peace one wants to build, one cannot easily define strategies and activities for peacebuilding interventions. It is very difficult to conduct a serious analysis of peacebuilding deficiencies when the end-goal is not known; in most cases, both intervening and local actors in conflict countries assume that everybody knows what peace is all about and therefore they leave the definition of and their vision for peace implicit. Because of this tendency, this step is very useful since it requires stakeholders to make their definition of and vision for an ideal type of peace explicit as they analyze current peacebuilding needs and consider intervention strategies (Boulding 2001, Dugan 2001, Fast and Neufeld 2005). This step is also important because values, objectives and visions are often based on different cultural, religious and theoretical backgrounds that need to be brought into the open and discussed before an agreed-upon framework for the intervention can be created (Lederach 2005; Avruch 1998).

In practice, several different sources and procedures can be used to assist in the visioning process and to specify interventions that are likely to enhance peacebuilding efforts:

– Using research results from scholars that analyze conditions for successful peacebuilding (see examples in chapter 12)
– Applying international norms and standards (see examples in chapter 12)
– Developing your own vision.

For a sector analysis, international norms and standards in the respective sector can be used to define the vision (e.g. ideal media, human rights or water supply situation) and compared to the current situation (e.g. current situation of the media, human rights or water supply in a given country). However, it is necessary to differentiate between peacebuilding interventions and those with other objectives; the sector analyzed for peacebuilding interventions is the *peace process*, whereas for development interventions the sector to be analyzed is health, education or water.

However, there are also sectors where it is difficult to find an analytical framework that is based on a broad consensus of peace and conflict-sensitive experts in that particular sector. Furthermore, sometimes in a peacebuilding intervention the stakeholders want to develop or promote their own vision for peacebuilding. In these cases, it is best to jointly develop your own vision of the ideal situation that can be compared with the current situation accordingly.

For development sector analysis – taking our example from SME development in Sri Lanka – we used a combination of soliciting opinions from sector and peacebuilding experts and a facilitated workshop of local stakeholders. We identified the peacebuilding needs in the respective sectors based on the analysis of what is needed to achieve peace and conflict sensitive SME development in the districts (see more in chapter 8).

*Step 4: Identifying and specifying the peacebuilding needs*

After the peacebuilding deficiencies have been analyzed, we can now specify the short, medium and long-term needs for peacebuilding by comparing the ideal situation (vision) with the reality on the ground.

The peacebuilding needs that will be addressed by an intervention form the basis for defining or assessing the intervention's goals, strategies and later activities.

20

In our example in Sri Lanka, the integration of the SME sector and the conflict and peace analyses led to the result that the equitable inclusion of the different Sri Lankan ethnic, language and religious groups (both refugees and local communities) into all activities of SME development was found as the main peacebuilding need, combined with promoting a business culture of working together.

## Assessing the Peacebuilding Relevance: Part 2

The aim of this next part of the 'Aid for Peace' framework is to assess whether the overall direction of a planned or ongoing intervention (policy, program, and project) corresponds to the country's peacebuilding needs as mapped in part 1.

The peacebuilding relevance assessment ensures the link between the analysis stage and the implementation of the intervention. It assesses the viability of the intervention's goals, e.g. whether or not the intervention has the potential of changing the situation in the desired manner; it stems from evaluation research and has been adapted to the use in the peace and conflict field. Thus, it is a unique methodological step that is not provided by any other existing peace and conflict related approach. Other approaches tend to skip the relevance question and move too quickly into assessing the effectiveness or impact of an intervention, rather than first finding out whether the intervention is relevant at all. In the planning phase of the intervention, the relevance assessment makes the future intervention more targeted; in the evaluation phase, it judges the relevance of ongoing interventions and suggests ways and means to improve the relevance for peacebuilding.

A peacebuilding relevance assessment is done by
a) comparing the objectives and main activities of the planned or existing intervention with the identified peacebuilding needs and
b) examining how and to what extend they are consistent with these needs. A relevance scale (see this scale in chapter 12) has proved to be a useful tool; and
c) avoiding duplicating other actors' past and present activities and incorporating lessons learned into the intervention design.

The latter is most often done through conducting a survey or appraisal about previous and current interventions made by other actors in the same sector. This is a particularly important step because it is difficult to judge the peacebuilding relevance of a single intervention for peacebuilding if we do not have information about all the other activities undertaken in the same sector. Moreover, intervening actors can learn from past mistakes and successes of other actors.

During the workshop for the Sri Lanka SME program, the stakeholders jointly defined sub-goals for the program to incorporate the peacebuilding needs and thus enhance the peacebuilding relevance. Specific guidelines for the selection of partners and beneficiaries were added to the implementation plan and contacts were established to other organizations working in the same.

## Assessing the Conflict Risks: Part 3

The objective is to identify the existing problems and risks which (the) intervention(s) in zones of armed conflict face, i.e. assessing or anticipating the effects the conflict has on the intervention. For planning new interventions, the conflict risk assessment anticipates potential conflict-related risks for the intervention. To assess the conflict risks, one can make use of a variety of checklists and methods (see our checklist in chapter 12 or Bush 2003). All checklists focus on questions relating to the security situation, the political and administrative climate, the relationship to partners and stakeholders, and the relationship to the parties in conflict and other intervening actors.

In our example from Sri Lanka, we analyzed a series of potential risks separately for every district based on the conflict/tension analysis done in the districts in question and checked it against our checklist to ensure that we had not missed anything. Later, during the development of the action plan (see further down), the stakeholders developed program recommendations (in the form of concrete activities to be implemented) in order to avoid these risks. The stakeholders of the intervention realized that some of the risks, like the escalation of violence, could not be influenced by the program pro-actively; however, a plan about how to deal with such a situation, should it arise, could be prepared in advance.

## Assessing the Conflict and Peacebuilding Effects: Part 4

The objective in this fourth part of the framework is to assess the effects (outcomes and impact) of the planned or ongoing intervention(s) on the conflict and peacebuilding situation. In other words, we want to translate our hypotheses of change into operational categories in order to find out what kind of intended effects can be expected in the future, what kind of effects are taking place at present, and/or what kind of effects have already taken place as a consequence of the intervention(s) both in terms of the immediate local and the wider conflict and peace situation(s). However, we also want to know potential, or real, unintended negative and positive effects. To ensure a proper assessment of peace and conflict effects, the two preconditions discussed below need to be considered.

First, a peacebuilding baseline study must be conducted prior to the intervention in order to include a before/after comparison as part of the overall assessment. According to the Glossary on Evaluation of the Development Assistance Committee (DAC) of the OECD (see http://www.oecd.org/dataoecd/29/21/2754804.pdf), a baseline study is an analysis describing the situation prior to an intervention, against which progress can be assessed or comparisons made at a later stage of the intervention. Our approach enriches typical baseline studies by adding requirements for working in conflict zones. At present, many actors intervening in a conflict situation conduct a conflict analysis. However, the peacebuilding baseline study included in 'Aid for Peace' provides much more detailed conflict analysis of the situation than is usually provided in other analyses. For example, once the peacebuilding needs have been identified, the peacebuilding baseline study provides details about the situation of different partners and beneficiary groups, their degree of participation in decision-making and peacebuilding, their affiliations to the conflicting actors, their membership bases, gender relations, or any other relevant issues that need to be defined. The peacebuilding baseline study can also be integrated into a normal development baseline, feasibility study, humanitarian or post-conflict needs assessment.

In case such a peacebuilding baseline study has not been conducted, assessors/ evaluators have to devise an assumed before/after comparison with the help of other tools, such as peacebuilding checklists or interviewing involved stakeholders and the wider constituency of the intervention about their perceptions of changes. It is, however, important to understand that these alternative methods can only approximate results.

Second, during the planning phase stakeholders need to make their hypotheses of change operational in agreeing on the results chains and indicators to be used for assessment purposes. Results chains and indicators facilitate the monitoring and evaluation of the effects of the intervention (see figure 6 and chapter 12 for details). In the field of development cooperation a set of standard indicators already exists. For example, the availability of clean water is an important indicator in assessing a country's health level. However, standard indicators are not available for all types of interventions. Peace research as a field is just beginning to explore a set of general indicators.

For planning new interventions we recommend developing hypotheses of change with the help of results chains that create causal links between the activities of the intervention(s) and the desired outcome/impact. This can be done with the help of a) participatory planning methods like Action Evaluation (Rothman 2003), b) ready-made checklists ('Do no Harm' and 'RPP' checklists on CDA (Collaborative for Development Action, http://www.cdainc.com); Bush 2003) and c) developing your own checklists. The latter can be done by using the results of the peacebuilding needs analysis and combining it with research results, sector knowledge and information from the ready-made checklists (see more in chapters 5, 8, 9).

Returning to the example of the SME program in Sri Lanka, we came up with a list of possible negative and positive effects the program could have on the conflict dynamics and peacebuilding process. Instead of merely giving recommendations, the stakeholders of the intervention jointly developed an action plan for incorporating the peace and conflict lens into the program implementation plan. During a facilitated workshop, the stakeholders checked all planned program implementation activities for their peace and conflict sensitivity and defined additional activities accordingly.

For existing interventions, in case no hypothesis and indicators were generated during planning, we strongly recommend engaging the intervention's stakeholders in such a process, even in the midst of an existing intervention. This will enable the intervention's staff and donors to better monitor outcomes and impact for the next phase of the project, program or policy intervention. Additional methods have to be applied to evaluations in these cases (see chapters 5 and 10).

For development interventions the different parts of the approach can also be integrated into standard planning or evaluation procedures (see chapters 9 and 10).

## Applying the 'Aid for Peace' Framework for Peacebuilding Interventions

For peacebuilding interventions the 'Aid for Peace' approach can be applied in the course of planning and for the evaluation of interventions during or after implementation. It can also be used for planning and assessment of the macro peace process interventions.

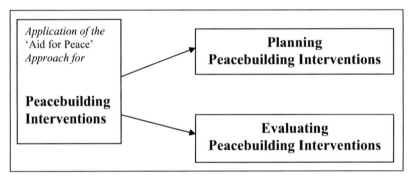

*Figure 2: The Application of the 'Aid for Peace' Approach*
*for Peacebuilding Interventions*

**Planning Peacebuilding Interventions:** This application purpose of the 'Aid for Peace' Approach has been developed for planning peace interventions on the policy or program level. This application will result in an implementation plan and a monitoring system for the respective intervention (see chapter 6).

**Evaluating Peacebuilding Interventions:** This application purpose of the 'Aid for Peace' approach has been specially developed for the evaluation of peacebuilding interventions. The user will get to understand what the precondition for evaluations are and how to systematically conduct an evaluation based on evaluation criteria and questions developed especially for peacebuilding interventions (see chapter 5).

## Applying the 'Aid for Peace' Framework for Development and Humanitarian Interventions

For development and humanitarian interventions, the 'Aid for Peace' approach can be applied during planning, for separate peace and conflict assessments, for evaluation during or after implementation, as well as for conflict monitoring. We distinguish three application forms in the diagram below.

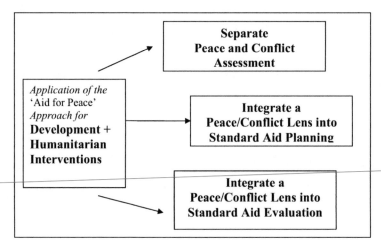

*Figure 3: The Application of the 'Aid for Peace' Approach for Aid Interventions*

**Conducting a Peace and Conflict Assessment:** This application is specifically designed for development and humanitarian interventions that have just passed the stage of standard aid planning or have already started implementation and would like to add the peace and conflict lens. Here the 'Aid for Peace' approach provides a separate assessment framework in addition to the standard planning procedures; its goal is to ensure that an intervention also looks into the peace and conflict relevance and effects in addition to the development or humanitarian goals. This application is comparable to environmental or gender assessments and seeks to add the peace and conflict dimension to the intervention's design and implementation (see chapter 8).

**Integrating a Peace/Conflict Lens into Standard Development Planning:** In contrast to the separate 'Aid for Peace' assessment, this application has been developed for those organizations that would like to shift to planning processes that integrate the peace and conflict lens throughout, instead of conducting a separate peace and conflict assessment. Here the user understands how to integrate the 'Aid for Peace' framework into the Project Cycle Management (PCM), a planning tool used by most aid agencies. This application is directed to organizations that are already familiar with the logical framework and planning procedures of the PCM or similar instruments. However, it is up to the specific aid agency to further adapt this general application to their specific planning procedures and needs (chapter 9).

**Integrating a Peace/Conflict Lens into Standard Aid Evaluation:** This application of the 'Aid for Peace' approach has been developed for organizations planning to conduct or commission a development or humanitarian evaluation of (an) aid intervention(s) taking place in situations of armed conflict or in the aftermath of a war or armed conflict. In this chapter, the user learns how to integrate the peace and conflict lens directly into standard evaluations along the DAC/OECD (Organization of Economic Cooperation and Development) and ALNAP (Active Learning Network on Accountability and Performance in Humanitarian Affairs) evaluation criteria by enriching these international agreed evaluation criteria, questions, methods and tools with the peace and conflict lens based on the 'Aid for Peace' framework (chapter 10).

## The Implementation Process

The 'Aid for Peace' approach requires a participatory implementation process that is focused on the needs of the intervention's stakeholders and owners. Good preparation is therefore essential! Stakeholders and owners jointly identify and discuss their needs during the preparation process and agree on an implementation plan for the application of the 'Aid for Peace' approach.

There is no best ready-made process, because each application form of the 'Aid for Peace' approach requires a different process. And, again, each process must be tailored to the needs of the respective intervention(s), its stakeholders and owners.

Nevertheless, there are some general process guidelines to follow. A good process design for applying the 'Aid for Peace' approach combines surveys or short studies, assessments and – most importantly – participatory planning and assessment methods involving all the relevant stakeholders and owners of the intervention throughout the process from the very beginning.

For planning new interventions, the main process takes place during a participatory planning workshop. However, prior to the workshop a peace and conflict analysis – as well as a more detailed peacebuilding baseline study – need to be conducted to prepare the ground for joint planning. For assessing or evaluating existing interventions, participatory workshops need to be combined with more field research.

Assessments are often conducted both at headquarters and in the field. It is most efficient to conduct studies or surveys prior to the field phase. Transparency about the process is required at all times; therefore both headquarters and field offices always need to be informed about the results of the different stages of the process.

# Part II

# Planning and Evaluating
# Peacebuilding Interventions

# 4   The Evolution of Peacebuilding Interventions and Current Challenges

## Towards professionalization of peacebuilding interventions

The international peacebuilding community is currently engaged in a debate about the professionalization, effectiveness and impact of peacebuilding interventions. The origins of this debate are to be found both in the evolution of the peacebuilding field as such as well as in the donor community's wish for more accountability and proof of impact of peacebuilding interventions. This part of the book is designed to contribute to further professionalization of the peacebuilding field by showing how to use the 'Aid for Peace' framework to better plan and evaluate peacebuilding interventions. In particular, the framework seeks to further these aims while preserving the core values of peacebuilding, such as working to transform armed conflicts into non-violent means for addressing concerns and strengthening capacities for social change.

In this part of the book, therefore, we want to show how peacebuilding interventions can be planned and evaluated. It is based on findings from our research on different aspects of peacebuilding; our experiences in applying and testing the 'Aid for Peace' framework for peacebuilding planning and evaluation processes over the last couple of years, and our activities supporting different donor agencies and NGOs in these endea-vors.

Before we explore peacebuilding planning and evaluation in detail, however, we wish to begin with a short overview of the history of peacebuilding. Our goal is to provide readers with a better understanding of why these issues are being discussed today and to lay the foundation for the remaining chapters within Part II of this book. After this introductory chapter, we move into a chapter on evaluation of peacebuilding interventions before discussing planning in the subsequent chapter. Logically, a chapter on planning would precede one on evaluation; however, we put the evaluation chapter first because a) the debate on peacebuilding evaluation has been established within the research, donor, and agency discourse whereas discussions on planning is still not widespread, and b) after reading about peacebuilding evaluation, it will be more clear that good planning is a prerequisite for good evaluation. Thus, by framing Part II in this manner, we hope to emphasize the interconnection between planning and evaluation to our readers.

## The institutionalization of modern peacebuilding

A variety of local and international actors have contributed to peacebuilding since ancient history, but it was only in the 20th century that means of peacefully resolving conflicts between states were institutionalized in international law. This process, which started with the 1898 Hague Peace Conference, included the creation of the League of Nations after World War I and was solidified with the foundation of the United Nations (UN) at the end of World War II. At this juncture, nation states and the UN were the actors with primary responsibility for monitoring and supporting world peace through mediation, facilitation, provision of good offices, and arbitration between states (Paffenholz 1998). Civil society involvement in peacebuilding, especially in international conflicts, was considered to complicate the efforts of professional diplomats (Paffenholz / Spurk 2006; Berman / Johnson 1977). Nongovernmental actors, such as the Quakers, were exceptions at that time (Curle 1971).

## The establishment of peace research as a discipline

Although individual scholars had long conducted peace research within a variety of academic disciplines, it was not until the 1960s that peace research was established as a normative, interdisciplinary academic field. Early peace theories focused on the analysis and practice of conflict management as well as on theories of nonviolent social and international change. However, peace research, in Europe as well as the United States, has always analyzed a wide array of causes for conflict, ranging from global, political, and economic issues to those dealing with religious, cultural, and social ones. During the Cold War, the prevention of a nuclear or conventional war between the two antagonist blocks became a main focus of peace research. Another, more recent, focus has been the 'democratic peace' debate, which links peace with democratic theory and builds on the early works of Kant (Kant 1781). One side of this debate concludes that democracies do not fight each other, a finding which is consequently used to justify both peaceful and military interventions aimed at democratization (Doyle 1983a, 1983b; Russett 1990; Brown et al. 1996).

## Increasing significance: The end of the Cold War and the 'UN Agenda for Peace'

The practice of peacebuilding only gained significant international momentum in the 1990s, at the end of the Cold War, as focus shifted away from wars between states to the management and resolution of armed conflicts within states (Miall et al. 1999; Eriksson et al. 2003). These debates were closely linked to the changing reality on the ground, which saw a significant increase of intrastate (internal) armed conflicts.

Such conflicts have accounted for approximately 80-90% of all conflicts since 1989 (Eriksson et al. 2003: 594).

Initially, interest in peacebuilding grew slowly, but the mid-1990s witnessed a rapid increase in peacebuilding activities. This increase went hand-in-hand with an international debate on the need to adapt international instruments to the new challenge of managing intrastate armed conflict. The UN Secretary General's 1992 report, 'An Agenda for Peace,' was the beginning of a still ongoing process of adaptation to the post-Cold War era (Boutros-Ghali 1992). This important document outlined a new framework for managing international conflicts. Not only was the term 'peacebuilding' introduced to the wider public, but the issue of post-conflict peacebuilding became a source of debate as the international community struggled to cope with the challenge of rebuilding societies after wars. In the early 1990s a number of armed conflicts were settled successfully, including those in Namibia, Angola, Mozambique, Cambodia, and El Salvador. Many thought the world would soon be free of armed conflict, as most of these intrastate conflicts had been Cold War proxy wars. However, the wars in Somalia and the former Yugoslavia combined with the genocide in Rwanda brought this short international euphoria to a harsh end.

## New debates after the Rwanda crisis

*Preventing armed conflicts: The early warning debate*

Since the 1994 Rwandan genocide, discussion about peacebuilding has intensified. This discussion first centered on the possibilities of preventing another situation like Rwanda from happening. This was the start of the political early warning discourse (Rupesinghe / Kuroda 1992). In the beginning of this debate it was assumed that within a couple of years quantitative methods would be available to precisely predict upcoming political violence and thereby enable the possibility for political early action. However, these hopes were not fulfilled because it became clear that quantitative early warning systems alone will not be able to predict political violence, and that lack of political willingness to engage in early action, not lack of information, was the main problem.

Thus, the early warning debate lost its momentum and was absorbed into the general debate about prevention culminating in the UN Secretary General's report from 2001 on 'Preventing Armed Conflict'. Nevertheless, today a number of quantitative as well as qualitative political early warning systems exist. While the International Crisis Group (ICG: www.icg.org) produces regularly qualitative analysis, a quantitative early warning system is run by the regional organization IGAD (Intergovernmental Agency for Development) in the Horn of Africa (www. cewarn.org).

The nexus between conflict, peace and development was first recognized in the early 1990s as development actors took on new tasks in response to the challenges of post-conflict peacebuilding. However, the issue only gained momentum in the aftermath of the tragic events in Rwanda, when research found that aid *can* do harm in conflict situations and may inadvertently have negative effects on conflict dynamics. Since this point the development community has been engaged in a series of debates about the linkages between peace, conflict and development (see chapter 7 for details).

The development community's involvement in the peacebuilding discourse has had several implications. First, many peacebuilding approaches and tools, such as conflict analysis frameworks, were imported into the development field. Second, the definition and understanding of peacebuilding has been stretched in terms of scope, duration, and content. In early 1990s, for instance, development actors first claimed that poverty reduction, and thus almost all development activities, contribute to long-term peacebuilding. Although by the end of the 1990s it became evident that poverty reduction alone does not automatically lead to more peaceful societies, most concurred that development *can* contribute to peacebuilding, albeit in different, more specific ways (see chapter 7). Third, development actors started to fund or implement interventions oriented towards direct peacebuilding. This contributed to increased activities, also gave rise to the professionalization and commercialization of peace work (Orjuela 2004; Pouligny 2005; Belloni 2001; Kaldor 2003).

## The mushrooming of peacebuilding initiatives

In the 1990s, the main discussion in research was which *external actors* would achieve the best results at ending armed conflict and wars with what kinds of approaches. The practice of peacebuilding during this time was characterized by testing many different approaches. Research has provided answers to a variety of detailed issues over the past ten years, resulting in the conclusion that only the involvement of a variety of different actors (including grassroots or other civil society actors) and approaches can lead to sustainable peacebuilding (for the state of debate see the three edited volumes of Reychler / Paffenholz 2001; Crocker et al. 2001 and Austin et al. 2004).

Contrary to the development discourse, the peacebuilding research debate remained focused on the role of external actors until the mid 1990s. The important work of John Paul Lederach shifted attention from external actors to the important role of actors from within the conflict country (Lederach 1997). This research led to a paradigm shift within the international practitioner community. From the mid-1990s onwards, external actors have moved from asking how they should be involved, to looking for ways to best support national conflict country actors in enhancing their peacebuilding capacities. The dissemination of this conceptual framework gave rise to and justification for the mushrooming of international, national, and local peace actors.

Today a wide array of non-state actors, such as NGOs, associations, religious entities, business and grassroots organizations, communities, or individuals are increasingly involved in different activities related to peacebuilding (Richmond / Carver 2005; Paffenholz / Spurk 2006; Goodhand 2006). Many different approaches and initiatives such as peace funds, dialogue projects, peacebuilding training, and capacity building programs for local actors have been tested during the last decade.

## Taking stock of experiences and lessons learned

### The 'Lessons Learned' debate

Since the start of the new millennium, practitioners and researchers have begun to take stock of a decade of practical experiences from countless peacebuilding interventions led by various actors in conflict zones around the world. Of particular concern is the issue of the impact of peacebuilding interventions on macro-level peace processes vis-à-vis the fact that the world seems no less peaceful than it was ten years ago. Consequently, the term 'lessons learned' entered the terminology of peace research and practice (Galama and van Tongeren 2002).

### Conditions for successful peace agreements

Most of the research findings to date focus on peace agreement successes and failures, i.e. identifying conditions for reaching sustainable peace agreements such as the willingness of rival leaders to compromise (Walter 1997); the ripeness of the conflict for resolution (Zartman 1989); the importance to deal with spoilers and hardliners that could challenge the entire process (Stedman 1997); the need to establish conflict resolution and power sharing institutions (Linder 1994); the importance of regional power balances; the existence of different mediation channels (Paffenholz 2001d, Fitzduff 2002), the quality of the peace agreement itself (Hampson 1996) and finally the cross-impact between the negotiation process, the agreement and the implementation (Reychler 2005).

### Post-conflict peacebuilding

The 'UN Agenda for Peace' established the importance of post-conflict peacebuilding in 1992. However, only towards the end of the last millennium did research begin to examine the experiences of almost a decade of post-conflict peacebuilding efforts. The main focus of this research was the durability of peace agreements, e.g. how can peacebuilding be sustained in the immediate aftermath of wars. We find two different discourses here:

The first discourse focuses on researching the conditions for successful implementation of post-conflict peacebuilding. Research found a number of such conditions that need to be in place for peace agreements to last such as power sharing agreements between the former conflicting parties, international commitment to the process, security guarantees or a good process design for the implementation of the peace agreement with suitable mechanisms like commissions for the regulation of unresolved issues (Stedman et al. 2002).

The second discourse criticizes the current international peacebuilding paradigm of 'liberal internationalism'. The paradigm of 'liberal internationalism' assumes that the best way to consolidate peace in war-shattered states is to transform the states into stable market democracies as quickly as possible. Critics argue, however, that the limited success of many post-conflict processes is because of the destabilizing effects generated by overly fast political and economic liberalization processes in post-conflict societies that do not meet the necessary preconditions (Paris 2004).

*Evaluation: effectiveness and impact of peacebuilding interventions*

The debate on lessons learned occurring within the field of peacebuilding since the late 1990s has recently matured with the consequence of shifting discussion toward the need to further professionalize intervention planning and evaluation. This discussion received further attention due to the donor community's reluctance in funding peace interventions that were not able to prove they made a positive impact on the peace process. Many peace interventions claim long-term impact on peace processes without being able to demonstrate these envisaged results. This seems to be of special concern for civil society peace process initiatives, as so many of them have received funds over the last decade. The Hewlett Packard Foundation, for example, one of the largest donors for research and NGO peace initiatives in the US, recently stopped this funding stream. Donor concerns have been expressed in numerous conferences and reports on the topic of evaluation in peacebuilding, and by the fact that many donors are currently drafting evaluation guidelines for peacebuilding interventions.

This was the start of the evaluation debate within peacebuilding. Contrary to the development field, where evaluation has long been a requirement for donor funds, the issue of evaluation has only recently entered the field of peacebuilding. Different projects have assessed peacebuilding experiences and a number of proposals and frameworks now exist that explain how to do peacebuilding evaluations (see chapter 5).

*Towards professionalization of peacebuilders*

The question about professionalism in the field of peacebuilding relates to the more professional planning, implementation and monitoring/evaluation procedures and tools (see above) as well as to the question of selecting the right people for peacebuilding. Whereas most professions have clear and generally accepted criteria for distinguishing qualified from unqualified practitioners, this remains lacking in the field of peacebuilding. Is a three day-, a weeklong- or three months training enough to send people to the field? Does an academic Master Program in Peace and Conflict Studies qualify someone for peace work? To further proceed with guidelines for good peacebuilders will not be an easy task, because it involves not only social and conceptual skills, but also requires motivation, talent, creativity, experience, leadership, and certain attitudes and values (Ingelstam 2001, Reychler and Stellamans 2005).

Beyond all debates about lessons learned, evaluation and professionalization, it is also important that the essential values and concepts of peacebuilding – the transformation of armed conflicts into peaceful means of social and political change – remain at the heart of peace work. However, these overall objectives can be better achieved by introducing more professional approaches and methods into the practice of peacebuilding. The professionalization of the peace field has already improved considerably during the past decade; however, work remains to be done. The following chapter thereby aims to contribute to the further professionalization of the peacebuilding field while also preserving the essential values of peacebuilding.

# 5 Evaluating Peacebuilding Interventions

The objective of this chapter is to provide an overview of the characteristics of peacebuilding evaluations by introducing guidelines that can be used by researchers, donors, implementing agencies, and evaluators to prepare for and conduct evaluations of peacebuilding interventions. The application of the 'Aid for Peace' approach to evaluating peacebuilding interventions has been developed by enhancing the existing 'Aid for Peace' framework with:

– Policy evaluation research (Patton 1997, Rossi et al. 1999);
– Evaluation in development cooperation and humanitarian aid (OECD/DAC guidelines, Kusek, Z.J. / Rist, R.C. 2004, ALNAP guidance);
– The debate on 'Peace and Conflict Impact Assessment' (PCIA) (see chapter 7);
– Evaluation concepts used in peacebuilding (Church / Shouldice 2002 and 2003, Smith 2003, Anderson / Olson 2003, Fast / Neufeld 2005);
– Peace research findings as well as 'lessons learned' and experience gleaned from peacebuilding practice (see chapter 4 for references);
– Three years of field testing (2002-2005) through peacebuilding program evaluations in the Horn of Africa, Congo, Sri Lanka, Nepal and Palestine; evaluations of two global Peace Funds, and evaluations of peacebuilding institutions in Europe.

Since evaluation is a newer debate within the field of peacebuilding, we first provide a general introduction to evaluation, and then outline the current debate regarding peacebuilding evaluations. Following this orientation to the subject, we move into the main focus of this chapter: a process design for peacebuilding evaluation, complete with guidelines, methods, tools, and helpful hints collected from field experience.

## What is evaluation?

Although there are many contending types of evaluation, the following definition encompasses all forms of evaluation, not just those for peacebuilding: An evaluation is a systematic assessment of policies, programs or institutions with respect to their conception and implementation as well as the impact and utilization of their results (Rossi et al. 1999).

Evaluation is used in almost all areas of life in theory and practice. In scientific research, for example, policy evaluation is an established discipline, which is concerned with the impact of public policies (Rossi et al. 1999; Bussmann et al. 1997). Evaluation is well established in the fields of development and humanitarian action, and international donors have agreed on a set of evaluation criteria that are applied as a matter of course (see evaluation weblinks in chapter 12).

An evaluation can have a number of different objectives simultaneously, such as:

- Reviewing and judging current status in order to improve current interventions
- Checking and controlling processes and procedures for purposes of accountability
- Assessing and documenting what has been achieved
- Identifying lessons learned for use in future interventions.

Evaluations can occur at any time during the implementation process. Usually evaluations are conducted in the middle of an intervention (mid-term review) or at the end (ex-post), depending on the objective of the evaluation (see above). Evaluations of long-term, complex programs or institutions can also take place periodically, starting shortly after the beginning of the implementation process, in order to further direct the intervention and allow for any necessary adjustments in course.

Essentially, there are two types of evaluations, formative and summative, which can be further divided into several subtypes. Formative evaluations seek insight into ways to improve the intervention in question, whereas summative evaluations assess and judge the intervention's quality and success in meeting its objectives. A summative evaluation is often carried out at the end of an intervention in order to document lessons learned and progress achieved.

Over the past few years, participatory and utilization-focused evaluation processes, including action evaluation, have become widespread. These processes involve primary stakeholders in the evaluation process, and emphasize the importance of stakeholders' ability to use the results for future improvement (Patton 1997). This approach reflects an orientation to evaluation that defines success in terms of how well the results can be used by those involved in the intervention. Furthermore, the participation of primary stakeholders in the evaluation process not only optimizes the use and acceptance of the results, but also contributes to joint institutional learning.

Evaluation research and practice draws on a set of criteria that are used to carry out an evaluation. Each evaluation criterion includes a number of questions and issues to be explored and addressed by the evaluator(s). These questions can be answered through the evaluators' application of different evaluation methods.

In evaluation practice, a set of 'standard criteria,' called such due to their use by most stakeholders in evaluation, are available for use in policy, development, or humanitarian evaluations. The OECD criteria and the European Commission's additional criteria are well known and widely used for the evaluation of development programs. An additional set of criteria for evaluating humanitarian action is provided by the Active Learning Network on Accountability and Performance in Humanitarian Affairs (www.alnap.org). With respect to peacebuilding, no widely agreed-upon set of criteria yet exists. However, since many peacebuilding interventions are funded by donors that also work in development, in practice many use the above mentioned criteria for peacebuilding interventions as well. The criteria to be used for a particular evaluation are decided when the evaluation is planned, i.e. when those involved in the planning of an evaluation stipulate which issues should be evaluated. In general, the criteria of 'relevance,' 'effectiveness,' 'impact,' and 'efficiency' are used in evaluating all types of interventions. Additional criteria used for development include 'sustainability,' 'coordination,' and 'coherence,' while the criteria of 'coverage' and 'protection' are often applied in humanitarian evaluations. 'Participation' is sometimes found in humanitarian evaluations as a criterion that assesses whether beneficiaries of interventions have been sufficiently involved in the implementation.

The following prerequisites are necessary before one can adequately conduct an evaluation:

– Clear and measurable objectives must be defined for the intervention, because interventions will be evaluated based on the extent to which they achieve these objectives. If the objectives are too vague, an accurate assessment will not be possible.
– A baseline study must be conducted prior to the intervention so that a before/ after comparison can be made as part of the evaluation. According to the OECD/ DAC Glossary (2002 see http://www.oecd.org/dataoecd/29/21/2754804.pdf), a baseline study is an analysis describing the situation prior to an intervention, against which progress can be assessed or comparisons made at a later stage of the intervention.
– Results chains and indicators are needed to assess the results of the intervention; these are the effects of the intervention on the immediate and larger context. Using information provided by the baseline study, the intervention's stakeholders will develop results chains and corresponding indicators for monitoring and evaluation purposes. A separate results chain is drawn up for each intervention objective and qualitative and quantitative indicators are defined for each link of the chain (see figure 6). Once results chains have been defined, internal monitoring and external evaluation become possible; the specified indicators can be used to assess each level of implementation, and the achieved results can be assessed by means of the indicators.

A word on indicators: although a standard set of indicators already exists in some fields, such as development, even within these fields there are some types of interventions for which indicators are not standardized. Furthermore, indicators have also to be developed for each part of the results chain, which requires careful thinking in order to develop appropriate criteria. For example, the level of education of women has been used to assess child health.

Which methods are used for an evaluation depends first and foremost upon the objective of the evaluation and the criteria to be analyzed. It also depends on the level of scientific rigor which is to be applied to an evaluation and the size of the available budget. In general, a combination of different social science and related methods are used, such as before/after comparisons, assessment of results chains and indicators based on data collected through a variety of tools including interviews of key stakeholders, representative surveys, and workshops with the participants.

An intervention's impact is determined by examining the larger changes initiated by the intervention within the general context, changes that often occur only after a longer time has passed. To attribute these changes to the intervention in question is often difficult as there may be many other reasons why certain changes have occurred. Such attribution problems are common in impact assessment and referred to as 'attribution gap' (see also chapter 12).

When assessing impact we are not only challenged by attribution problems, but also by the fact that donors often think in-depth social science research is not cost-effective. Without serious research, however, it is impossible to assess impact, which most donors require funding recipients to demonstrate. One option for overcoming this problem is to engage in multi-actor impact assessments of entire countries or regions. For example, a year after the Tsunami earthquake in Sri Lanka, a coalition of organizations has begun to conduct joint evaluations of the effects of the Tsunami aid (Tsunami Evaluation Coalition (TEC)).

If the above-mentioned prerequisites for evaluation are not fulfilled, evaluators have to work with assumed results chains and before/after comparisons through surveys or group discussions with stakeholders in order to assess the approximate results of the intervention.


## Evaluation in Peacebuilding

The issue of evaluation has only recently entered the field of peacebuilding (see chapter 4). The report entitled 'The Evaluation of Conflict Resolution Interventions' (Church / Shouldice 2002) provides a good overview of the subject matter up to and including 2002. In the past few years, several programs not explicitly entitled 'evaluation' have assessed peacebuilding experiences, such as the 'Joint Utstein Study' (Smith 2003), which analyzed the peacebuilding efforts of several governments, and the 'Reflecting on Peace Project (RPP)', which evaluated lessons learned from NGO peacebuilding efforts (Anderson / Olson 2003). The Nairobi Peace Initiative also assessed its own experience with peacebuilding in Kenya in the late 1990s and developed a 'Framework for Learning and Assessment' (Galama / Tongeren 2002).

Studies, such as 'Confronting War' (Anderson / Olson 2003), provide important lessons learned for those evaluating peacebuilding interventions. 'Confronting War' presents the results of the RPP project, focusing primarily on how to ensure and finally evaluate the impact of peacebuilding interventions on the macro-level peace process (which they call 'peace writ large'). Although the authors only touch on the subject of evaluation, they have identified important questions which should be considered by those evaluating peacebuilding interventions. A 2005 thematic issue of the 'Journal of Peacebuilding and Development' (Vol. 2, No.2) focuses on evaluation and gathers together a collection of articles that include both general and more specific approaches to peacebuilding evaluation, as well as a few integrated approaches to development/peacebuilding evaluations. A number of US based NGOs have published guidelines for monitoring and evaluation of NGO conflict transformation programs (Church / Rogers 2006). The OECD Development Assistance Committee is currently in a process to develop guidelines for the evaluation of conflict prevention and peacebuilding interventions.

At the nexus of peacebuilding and development, we find interesting proposals linking debates about social change and conflict transformation with those surrounding development effectiveness. However, most learning in this field to date has been gained from case study evaluations and much of the information is not conducive to building a common guidance for evaluation. Several problems pose challenges to building upon peacebuilding evaluation experience for the purpose of institutional learning. First, many existing evaluations are not available to the general public because they remain with the commissioning donors or agencies. Another problem stems from the fact that many evaluation reports seldom make their methodological approaches transparent or else have such different conceptional starting points from each other that they cannot be compared.

Donors, organizations, and evaluators face similar problems when evaluating peacebuilding interventions. A few of these problems are discussed below:

**Values versus tools:** Peacebuilding actors often resist evaluation because they fear that the essential goals of peacebuilding – transforming armed conflicts into peaceful means of managing disputes and encouraging social change – can simply not be measured because they are not technical issues.

**Evaluation versus Research:** Peace researchers sometimes argue that the current debate on evaluation misses the mark as more serious research on the effects of peacebuilding interventions is more important than conducting evaluations. While peace research *is* needed, the argument is often based on a misperception of evaluation and is due in part to the blurry distinction between evaluation and research, especially in terms of assessing outcomes and particular impact (the job of social science research). Many wrongly equate evaluation with poorly conducted evaluations reliant on quickly rushed processes. Indeed, there is a danger that many evaluations are implemented in a quick and rushed manner; however, this does not discredited the concept of evaluation as such. Especially in the fields of development and humanitarian action, a very professional discussion about standard evaluation criteria and best practices is on-going. If organizations fail to exploit this available information it is not the fault of evaluation as a concept. We have, however, found insufficient research-oriented evaluations as well as a lack of evaluation-oriented research projects, especially when it comes to impact assessment. Consequently, peace research should better collaborate with donors and agencies in order to encourage research-oriented studies that complement impact assessments. Such paired projects could, for example, focus on an entire country program of one or more donors, or could examine all interventions in a given area. At the same time, more evaluation-oriented research should be conducted in order to learn more about the impact of peace interventions in general.

**Focus on macro-level impact – more modest claims:** To assess impact is generally the most difficult task in evaluation research and practice due to attribution problems and the often costly procedures and methods for solid impact assessment. However, the debate on evaluation in the peacebuilding field tends to focus on assessing the impact of interventions on the macro-level. Actors try hard to find the link between, for example, a peace journalism training project and change in the peace process. While we believe that it is necessary for intervening actors to ask themselves how their intervention will affect 'peace writ large' before they begin, we wonder whether every given intervention needs to reach the top. Shouldn't impact depend more on the specific objectives of an intervention rather than macro-level indicators? We assert that one of the main problems in the peacebuilding evaluation field is that peace actors too often set overly ambitious objectives for their interventions. If program objectives are set in high, overly general terms such as 'achieving peace writ large,' then it is only fair to look for the impacts of the intervention on peace writ large. However, it might be better to focus on the intervention's relevance for peacebuilding first (Are we doing the right thing?) and only after relevance has been established should we look for a link between the intervention and its possible impact. For example, the objective of a peace journalism training could be reformulated from 'contributing to peacebuilding in country X through peace journalism' to the more modest goal of 'changing stereotypes in conflict reporting to contribute to more accurate reporting that thereby change peoples' attitudes of the 'other'.' However, before even this goal could be set, one should assess the relevance of such an intervention for peacebuilding by asking whether such an intervention is appropriate for that particular country at this very moment. As a case in point, in a country where journalists are constantly threatened by conflict parties and jailed if they report on certain issues, such an intervention is not timely. Instead, other measures, such as protection programs for journalists or the application of political pressure on the conflict parties might be more appropriate.

**The key to good evaluation is good planning.** Most peace organizations have not yet established professional planning procedures, which further complicates evaluation. Thus, a discussion about better planning in peacebuilding interventions might be more useful in the short term as a necessary step preceding the discussion about evaluation (see chapter 6).

Many of the *prerequisites* for evaluation listed earlier *are not sufficiently fulfilled* in peacebuilding.

a. Many peacebuilding programs pursue only very general objectives, such as 'making a contribution to peace', which cannot be evaluated due to their vague, all-encompassing nature. For this reason, more specific objectives are required (see example above).

b. Although compiling a more or less comprehensive analysis of a country's or region's conflict dynamics and peace process has now become an established practice of many peace organizations, these analyses often do not suffice as baseline studies to conduct a Before/After comparison at a later stage. To stick with the peace journalism example above – if no data is available regarding the quality of journalistic reporting before the project was initiated, it is very difficult to assess at a later stage what changes the project has actually achieved in the reporting style.

c. Most peacebuilding programs do not yet include results chains with indicators in their planning as a means to make their hypotheses of change operational (see figure 6). This makes reliable assessment of the effects of the intervention (immediate outcomes and wider impact) difficult.

**Participation of local actors versus external evaluation:** Peace practitioners often argue that external evaluations tend to ignore the knowledge of local actors. Such omission is particularly problematic in the peace field since this is the population the intervention seeks to empower. However, this assumption seems to be based partly on lack of knowledge about evaluating procedures and processes. Today standard evaluation procedure involves local actors on the evaluation team as well as in the evaluation process through participatory workshops, briefings, and de-briefings.

## The Uniqueness of Peacebuilding Evaluations?

Prior to presenting guidelines for the evaluation of peacebuilding policies and programs, we need to clarify any distinguishing factors between peacebuilding and other evaluations. Are peacebuilding evaluations unique? In the course of our evaluations of a wide variety of peacebuilding programs, policies, and institutions we applied different criteria and methods to investigate this matter. After this testing, we arrived at the conclusion that most of the standard criteria for evaluation, especially those for policy evaluation research and development, can also be used for peacebuilding evaluation. However, we also found that most of these criteria need to be adapted to the specific peacebuilding situation and that others need to be added to the list. In addition, we concluded that existing evaluation methods and tools can be used equally as well for peacebuilding evaluations. In sum, it is not the 'how do we evaluate' that differs, but the specific criteria, or the particular meaning of a standard criterion when applied in peacebuilding evaluation.

A crucial issue for peacebuilding evaluations involves defining the peace one wants to realize and articulating the necessary preconditions for that vision. For many peacebuilding programs and policies, both the definition of peace and the underlying theoretical assumptions about building peace remain implicit. This poses a problem for evaluators as the intervention's goals remain fuzzy. It is very difficult to evaluate the relevance, effectiveness, or impact of a peacebuilding policy or program on the peace process when we do not know what kind of 'peace' they sought to build and what their hypotheses of change had been. The development field used to face a similar problem, but has spent decades discussing what poverty, and thus poverty reduction, is all about and has developed (over many years) a set of indicators to measure poverty. This discussion has not yet taken place to the same extent in the peace field. Although the famous peace researcher Johan Galtung has distinguished between negative peace (absence of war) and positive peace (society without direct and structural violence) since his early works, there is to date no understanding of how this positive peace can be achieved or what exactly it looks like. While positive peace is an ideal that will never fully be implemented, common understanding in the field asserts that the road to positive peace requires conflict transformation and social change (Lederach 1997). However, there is no agreement on the precise path of that road, and different schools of thought offer a variety of suggestions regarding how to transform armed conflict into peaceful means of resolving disputes (Miall et al. 1999). The lack of systematic debate on this matter within the field proves to be an obstacle for peacebuilding evaluations; achievements cannot be evaluated without a clear vision of or idea for what kind of peace should be built.

Peacebuilding evaluations also differ from other evaluations in terms of the specific context – conflict and peacebuilding – that should be influenced by the intervention. While other evaluations also need to analyze their respective contexts, armed conflicts are incredibly complex social and political phenomena that require special attention and in-depth analysis. Peacebuilding processes are also intensely vulnerable, making them difficult to assess in the short run; ultimately, only sustainable peacebuilding counts as success. Thus, it is necessary to evaluate whether current interventions are on the right road to contribute to sustainable peacebuilding. This may sound similar to development evaluations; however, the stakes are much higher. When peacebuilding interventions fail, the recurrence of violence has tremendous negative implications on the lives of generations of people.

To summarize, peacebuilding interventions have some special characteristics that need to be taken into account for evaluation purposes, but peacebuilding does not require a unique form of evaluation. One of the most important issues when considering peacebuilding evaluation, however, is ensuring the right process design.

## The Evaluation Process

The practice of evaluation in peacebuilding is relatively new and has not yet been generally accepted by peace actors. Practical experience has shown that evaluation can be an accepted, constructive instrument for learning, especially when those involved in the evaluation approach it as an opportunity for improving the success of the intervention, rather than regarding it as an instrument of donor control. Evaluation processes that make use of a combination of participatory and utilization-focused procedures are especially suited for achieving this objective.

Utilization-focused evaluation is a type of evaluation that seeks to provide results that are of immediate benefit for those who are directly involved in the intervention (Patton 1997). The utilization-focused aspect of an evaluation is generally ensured by defining clear utilization-focused objectives and by involving all relevant actors in planning the evaluation as well as in subsequent implementation of follow-up processes.

Participation of all actors is ensured by so-called participatory evaluation processes that involve all stakeholders and owners of the intervention. In this way, evaluation can also make a contribution to peacebuilding in itself as the process becomes a shared learning experience for the participants. It is important that donors and members of implementing agencies (headquarters and field staff), as well as local partners and external evaluators, are included in all the stages of the process, from planning to implementation up to evaluation.

## Seven Steps for Good Process Design for Peacebuilding Evaluations

### Step 1: Decision to conduct the evaluation

The process for implementing an evaluation of peace interventions starts – as do all evaluations – with the decision to conduct the evaluation. This decision is made mostly by donors, but it should nevertheless be discussed and jointly agreed upon by both donor and implementing agency. At the time this decision is made, it is already important to agree on the *type* of evaluation to be conducted.

### Step 2: Developing the 'Terms of Reference'

After the decision to evaluate has been made, the next step requires developing the Terms of Reference (TOR) for the evaluation (see a checklist in chapter 12). This step is particularly important for peacebuilding interventions as involved stakeholders are often not familiar with evaluations. Important issues that need to be considered include: the objectives of the evaluation (in order to ensure that results will be used); the evaluation criteria to be assessed; the detailed evaluation process, and the tasks and management responsibilities for each stage of the evaluation process. It is important that all relevant actors are involved (representatives from donors, implementing agencies, partners and evaluators) in the drafting of the TOR and that they agree to it. Partners and other involved actors are also involved in this process through participatory briefing and debriefing workshops before and after the evaluation mission as well as through group discussions during the mission.

The composition of the evaluation team is also crucial to establish at this time. In order to ensure participation and the focus on the usefulness of evaluations, it is a good idea to have a mixed evaluation team comprised of both external (foreign) and local evaluators. Whether or not insiders from the organization being evaluated and from the donor agency should be integrated into the evaluation team remains an issue under debate; the decision to include such insiders depends in part on the objective and type of the evaluation. In case the primary objective of an evaluation is accountability, it is best to have a team comprised of independent external evaluators. However, if the primary objective is to improve the intervention, such as when planning for a next phase, the participation of an insider from the organization as an additional evaluation team member can be considered. Those who argue against including insiders feel this casts doubt on the independence of the results; those in favor of including insiders suggest it leads to better follow-up and use of the evaluation results (please refer to team selection criteria in chapter 12).

*Step 3: Internal self evaluation*

It is advantageous to lay the groundwork for an external evaluation by conducting an internal evaluation of the intervention by its stakeholders. The group leading the internal evaluation can be a program management team or be comprised of a broader array of owners and stakeholders. The process provides a time for self-reflection and allows the team to assess its own intervention, which promotes a culture of learning and evaluation. Furthermore, it can produce valuable information to facilitate the external evaluation process to come. The internal evaluation can look into specific aspects only or may investigate all relevant evaluation criteria (see below). To implement a self-evaluation properly, stakeholders should follow approximately the same guidelines as apply to evaluation in general.

*Step 4: Evaluation process at headquarters*

After the results of the self-evaluation are available, the external evaluation can begin. The actual implementation of an evaluation begins at the headquarters of donors and implementing agencies before moving to the field. It is important to involve all relevant stakeholders and not only those commissioning the evaluation.

*Step 5: Field mission*

Pending on the location, scope, and objectives of the particular peacebuilding interventions to be evaluated, a mission to the field is usually needed. During such a field mission important process issues need to be considered, including ensuring the participation of all relevant field actors (field staff of donors, agency and local partners and relevant external stakeholders). The evaluation team should hold a joint briefing with all involved stakeholders before the agreed-upon evaluation process for the field mission starts. At the end of the field mission, the evaluation team's preliminary findings should be presented and discussed with all relevant stakeholders during a participatory workshop. Whether or not recommendations should already be presented during this workshop, or whether they should be written by the evaluators afterwards in light of the discussions, depends on the specific evaluation process.

*Step 6: De-briefing at headquarters*

During this step the findings of the evaluation team and the results of joint discussions at the field workshop will be presented and discussed with the stakeholders from headquarters. Their additional comments and recommendations will be incorporated later into the evaluation report.

*Step 7: Reporting and Dissemination*

Once all of these meetings with the various stakeholders have been completed, the evaluation team writes the evaluation report along the evaluation criteria (see chapter 12). When the draft report is finalized, it is sent to all relevant stakeholders at headquarters and in the field for feedback. The evaluation team incorporates comments and finalizes the report.

The final report is sent to all involved stakeholders. The TOR usually specifies to whom exactly the report has to be sent. It is up to the commissioning donor or agency to distribute the evaluation report to an even wider audience; this target group is often agreed on in the beginning of the process. Many organizations nowadays use the internet as an alternate means of publishing the report, either in part or in its entirety. This is an important step for the field of peacebuilding as such evaluations serve as important learning tools for other organizations.


## The Evaluation Framework

Earlier in this chapter we discussed internationally agreed-upon criteria for evaluations and noted that both the development and peacebuilding communities have developed criteria for evaluating their activities.

Combining criteria drawn from the policy evaluation, peace research, international experiences in development and humanitarian action, and peacebuilding evaluations with our own field testing, we integrated our standard 'Aid for Peace' framework into a set of evaluation criteria necessary for the evaluation of peacebuilding interventions. The following criteria are suitable for the evaluation of peacebuilding interventions:

1. Peacebuilding Relevance
2. Peacebuilding Effectiveness
3. Impact on Macro Peacebuilding
4. Sustainability for Long-Term Peacebuilding
5. Participation and Ownership of National/Local Stakeholders
6. Coordination and Coherence with other Initiatives
7. Efficiency, Management and Governance.

The following section presents these criteria, gives guidelines on how to apply them and provides accompanying evaluation questions, methods, tools, and examples from our field testing. The text below explains the breakdown used for each criterion:

a. The meaning of each criterion for evaluation in peacebuilding;
b. The main evaluation questions to be assessed by the evaluation team for every criterion (here we have enriched evaluation questions from development and policy evaluation research with relevant questions from peace research and peacebuilding evaluations);
c. Useful evaluation methods as used in evaluation research;
d. Practical tools that are commonly used for evaluations and in social science research, and
e. Hints and examples from peacebuilding evaluations in the field.

## 1. Peacebuilding Relevance

*a) Meaning of the criterion:*

The relevance criterion is used to assess the significance of the intervention for peacebuilding, i.e. to what extent the objectives and activities of the intervention(s) respond to the needs of the peacebuilding process. The peacebuilding relevance links the analysis of the conflict situation and the peacebuilding process with the intervention's objectives and thus seeks to find out whether an intervention is on the right track to contribute to peacebuilding. In order to find out the relevance of an intervention for peacebuilding, it is also necessary to assess what other actors are present and whether past interventions have had similar objectives. We want to know whether an intervention is forming part of a building block for peacebuilding, e.g. whether it is comprehensive.

*b) Evaluation questions:*

– Do the objectives and essential intervention's activities correspond with the needs of the peacebuilding process?
   Have the interventions' stakeholders developed or made explicit a clear and compelling vision for peacebuilding?
– Have the intervention's stakeholders developed the intervention's objectives according to this vision?
– Have the right actors been influenced?
– Has the intervention acknowledged present and past interventions of other actors (successes and failures) into the planning and implementation process and have developed the intervention's objectives and main activities in line with other actors' activities in order to contribute to comprehensive peacebuilding?

*c) Evaluation methods:*

Peacebuilding Relevance Assessment (see 'Aid for Peace' framework chapters 2 and 12 for details)

*d) Evaluation tools:*

The relevance assessment is best being conducted as a combination of the following tools:
– Study of intervention documents;
– Interviews with key stakeholders;
– Survey or group discussion with other actors with similar past and present interventions
– Participatory stakeholder workshop using the relevance scale (see chapter 12).

*e) Hints from field experience*

During field testing we experienced that the relevance/comprehensiveness assessment can be done both as desk work or as a participatory exercise or as a combination. For example, when evaluating a joint donor countrywide Peace Fund in Nepal that is aimed at supporting civil society peace actors, an assessment of the peace and conflict situation as well as a peacebuilding baseline study of the situation of civil society in Nepal had been conducted at the beginning of the intervention two years earlier. Moreover, in the meantime the involved stakeholders had conducted a mini-survey of the support different international donors gave to peace organizations in Nepal. As all this information already existed, the evaluation team, which was comprised of international and local peace and evaluation experts, just updated the situation analysis. Thus, the relevance assessment could be done at a desk by simply comparing the current situation with the previous one and assessing whether the interventions were still relevant for peacebuilding in Nepal. At the debriefing workshop in the field, the results were presented and discussed with the involved stakeholders. The evaluation team adapted the relevance assessment in light of the debate. It then became part of the evaluation report.

Another approach was chosen for an evaluation of a peacebuilding program in the Horn of Africa: here it was jointly decided by the evaluators and the implementing organization to conduct the relevance assessment during a participatory stakeholder workshop as a joint learning exercise. This proved to be very helpful as the involved stakeholders were able to reach a common understanding of the root causes of the conflict; articulate their vision for peacebuilding, and clearly understand why they were planning certain activities. They also understood and accepted that not all the program activities were relevant for peacebuilding. For example, they had assumed that peace journalist training for newspaper journalists was needed. However, they had never conducted a peacebuilding baseline study prior to the intervention that would have provided them with the information that a) most journalists were lacking basic journalist skills and would need this basic training first, and b) the primary media outlets were radio stations and not newspapers, and c) the selection of articles was solely done by the editors and not by the journalists themselves. Thus, their peace education training was relevant in the long run, but not under the given circumstances and not for the newspaper journalists they had chosen. In order to make the program more relevant for peacebuilding, it was jointly decided to develop new training courses along the immediate needs for peacebuilding for the second phase of the program, e.g. engaging in cooperation with a media training institution to provide basic journalistic training first, followed by peace education training for radio journalists and their editors.

## 2. Peacebuilding Effectiveness

*a) Meaning of the criterion:*

This criterion is used to evaluate whether an intervention has reached its objectives, which requires identifying the outcomes of the intervention with respect to its immediate peacebuilding environment. The key to evaluating effectiveness and thus the linkage between outputs/outcomes and impacts (see figure 6 and chapter 12), is finding out the degree to which the envisaged objectives have been fulfilled and noting changes that the intervention has initiated in its immediate peacebuilding environment. These changes should be the desired changes the intervention wanted to achieve (=objective of the intervention) as well as unintended positive changes.

*b) Evaluation questions:*

- To what extent were the objectives achieved / are likely to be achieved?
- What were the major factors influencing the achievement or non-achievement of the objectives?
- What process of desired change has the intervention initiated in its immediate peacebuilding environment?

*c) Evaluation methods:*

There are different methods which can be easily combined or applied in parallel in order to answer the questions above:

– Before/after comparison (ideally with the help of data from the baseline study)
– Evaluation of the objectives achieved by checking the results chains with the indicators (see chapter 12); ideally these results chains have been developed during planning. This is often not the case in the evaluation of peacebuilding interventions, in which case it is necessary to work with assumed results chains, see example below).

*d) Evaluation tools:*

– Strengths/weakness analysis for all objectives and activities with participants in a workshop;
– Assessing the perceptions of stakeholders in the immediate environment of the intervention through public perception surveys conducted with a representative sample of stakeholders;
– Interviews with key stakeholders assessing their perceptions;
– Quantitative and qualitative social science data collection.

*e) Hints from field experience*

During field testing we found that assessing outcomes is not an easy task since most interventions we evaluated neither had conducted a peacebuilding baseline study prior to the intervention nor had they developed results chains and indicators for monitoring and evaluation purposes. Thus the basic preconditions for assessing outcomes were not present. In fact, most organizations we worked with were not even aware of the advantage of a proper planning process as a means of creating the preconditions for monitoring and evaluating. Most organizations had monitoring systems in place, but they mainly focused on reporting outputs, like listing the number of training courses they had conducted. This reduced the monitoring reports basically to activity reports. When we asked organizations how they know whether they have reached their objectives, they often answered: 'This will show only after a longer period of time'. For example, the organization with the journalist peace education training program aimed at changing the attitudes of conflicting parties by training journalists how to do peace journalism in reporting without stereotypes of the conflicting parties. For assessing the output of these training, it was sufficient to check the activity reports of the organization that showed the number of conducted courses. However, for assessing the outcome of the training, we needed to know whether the journalists actually used the new reporting skills they had learned during the peace journalism training. In order to arrive closer to the outcomes, we first interviewed a representative sample of the former trainees. Most of them said that the training was very helpful, however when they changed their reporting style, they were criticized by their editors and their articles were rarely published. The question for us as an evaluation team became how we could get more detailed information about their reporting. The only way to find this out was through a proper content analysis of the newspaper articles they had written before and after the training. As we had not planned this beforehand, we were only able to carry out a rapid appraisal of a small number of sample articles, which we did in cooperation with a local journalist training institution. The result pointed to the fact that the style of reporting in most articles had not changed. This was an interesting finding as it contrasted with the perceptions of the journalists themselves! As mentioned previously, our evaluation of this program led to the stakeholders jointly deciding to change the program in its next phase. The organization also decided to build additional activities for monitoring outcomes into the program design for the next phase, such as initiating a cooperative effort with the local media institution for content analysis of representative samples. In order to ensure the quality of the analysis, they also included content analysis training for the new partner organization into their program as a new activity.

### 3. Impact on Macro Peacebuilding

*a) Meaning of the criterion:*

This criterion is used to identify and evaluate the effects the intervention has had on the larger peacebuilding and conflict environment, i. e. assessing the micro/macro link.

*b) Evaluation questions:*

−   Have processes and initiatives been instigated which have had an effect upon the macro-level peacebuilding process?

*c) Evaluation methods:*

There are different methods which can be easily combined or applied in parallel in order to answer the questions above. The methods and tools are almost similar to those used for assessing effectiveness (see above and chapter 12):
−   Before/after comparison, ideally with the help of data from the baseline study or with other tools
−   Evaluation of the objectives achieved by checking the results chains with the indicators.

*d) Evaluation tools:*

For single interventions:
−   Strengths/weaknesses analysis for all objectives and activities with participants in a workshop using the RPP questions (http://www.cdainc.com/)
−   Assessing the perceptions of stakeholders with regard to change in the larger

environment through public perception surveys conducted with a representative sample of stakeholders
- Interviews with key stakeholders assessing their perceptions of the micro-macro link.

For multi-stakeholder interventions:

- Public opinion polls and surveys with respect to changes (pending on the intervention's objectives e.g. attitudes, behaviors)
- Applied social science research.

*e) Hints from field experience*

One evaluation that we conducted during our field testing involved assessing the impact of the work of the Life and Peace Institute (LPI), a Swedish institution that ran peacebuilding, leadership, and transformation training courses in Somalia over a period of almost ten years (Paffenholz 2003). When interviewing the participants of the Somali peace negotiations in Aarta in 2001, researchers found out that more than 60% of all participants had been LPI trainees. Thus the micro-macro link of the training could be successfully evaluated.

More information on the impact of international support to conflict-affected Palestinian regions in Gaza and the West Bank is provided by a research project of the Institute for Development Studies of the University of Geneva. The researchers have developed a comprehensive approach for assessing the impact of aid that investigates the living conditions of the respective population twice a year using social-science research methods such as public perceptions surveys. The reports provide important insights into the requirements of the population in terms of the conflict situation and the impact of the aid. The members of the donor consortium financing the project use the data and analysis to tailor their programs towards the needs of the population. This example clearly shows that such an effort is only cost effective if a couple of actors join hands for impact assessment (please see: http://www.unige.ch/iued/new/palestine/).

## 4. Sustainability for Long-Term Peacebuilding

*a) Meaning of the criterion:*

This criterion is used to evaluate whether the intervention could help to create the conditions for long-term peacebuilding. To assess sustainability is not just something peacebuilding evaluation should take over from development because it seems to be a good practice. Rather, sustainability is a crucial criterion for peacebuilding. From peace research we know that peacebuilding processes are long-term and thus need long-term engagement to be successful. This long-term engagement can only be achieved through either a real long-term engagement of an organization in the field or through a strategy to sustain the intervention's results after the end of the intervention (Lederach 1997; Paffenholz 2003).

*b) Evaluation questions:*

– Which steps have been taken or are planned to create long-term processes, structures and institutions for peacebuilding?
– Have peacebuilding interventions of a short-term nature included measures which permit a transition to longer-term institution-building interventions of peacebuilding or democratization?
– Has a meaningful 'handing over' strategy been developed to local partners or actors that enable these partners to build their own peacebuilding initiatives?

*c) Evaluation methods:*

Assessment of changes initiated in institutional structures including the effectiveness of such changes.

*d) Evaluation tools:*

– Assessment of the intervention program documents
– Workshops with stakeholders
– Interviews with key stakeholders

*e) Hints from field experience*

We evaluated the sustainability of a huge peace program in Africa. Here the international NGO actually stayed in the field for almost ten years, had trained many local trainers that were working for the organization in the field, and started to establish a good handing-over strategy to several newly created local entities. At first glance sustainability seemed to be a given; after a second look, when interviewing other local organizations and the stakeholders of the intervention, we realized that the handing over process was not as excellent as originally thought. The local entities depended (financially and work-wise) on the international agency and were not operating as independent structures. Another example comes from Afghanistan, where an international NGO had supported a national civil society peace network. From the very beginning of the intervention, a sustainability strategy was developed and a smooth and short handing-over process that included capacity building and developing ownership resulted in an effective national entity after only three years. These examples show that we must look more closely when assessing sustainability and that we also need to assess the effectiveness of the structures that should lead to sustainability.

## 5. Participation and Ownership of National/Local Stakeholders

*a) Meaning of the criterion:*

These criteria are used to evaluate whether the relevant actors have been involved in the intervention's planning and implementation and whether meaningful local and national capacities for peacebuilding have been created and are owned by the national/local stakeholders.

*b) Evaluation questions:*

− Have the most important program partners and owners been involved in planning and implementation? The 'do-no-harm' and/or RPP questions can be applied here as well as gender criteria i.e. (see http://www.cdainc.com):
− How have local peace capacities been supported in the context of planning and implementation?
− Have local partners and owners been supported in order to develop their own structures and initiatives?
− Have those involved been selected according to the criteria of inclusiveness, inter-group fairness, and gender-balance?
− Have the partners and beneficiaries been able to initiate their own peacebuilding activities?

*c) Evaluation methods:*

Assessment of degree of participation and ownership.

*d) Evaluation tools:*

− Study of intervention documents
− Workshops and interviews with relevant stakeholders.

*e) Hints from field experience*

In our experience, the degree of meaningful participation in and ownership of an intervention can already be seen during the discussion about the evaluation process that occurs before the development of the 'Terms of Reference' for the evaluation. Usually organizations that have a participatory culture will involve all relevant actors and expend a lot of effort to ensure that the evaluation will have sufficient time to include the stakeholders and owners of the intervention. In addition, the degree of participation can also be seen through the invitation list of participatory stakeholder workshops However, participation itself is not a neutral or 'good' objective per se, but requires an in-depth look throughout the implementation to ensure fair representation. We found out that some of the 'do no harm' checklist questions (see CDA: http://www.cdainc.com) provide a good tool for assessing the peace and conflict sensitivity level of participation. In an evaluation in Sri Lanka the level of participation of local people in decision making in the interventions we evaluated was very high, however, only locals from one ethnic group were participating due to simple reasons such as language and professional skills.

## 6. Coordination and Coherence with other Initiatives

*a) Meaning of the criteria:*

These criteria are used to evaluate the level of coordination and coherence of the intervention with respect to the interventions of other actors since peacebuilding successes can only be achieved if coherence with other interventions is ensured (Fitzduff 2001, Paffenholz 2001d).

*b) Evaluation questions:*

– Are other peacebuilding actors in the country working towards the same objectives and objectives?
– Have the different activities been planned and implemented coherently?
– Has cooperation between the peacebuilding donors and organizations been institutionalized?
– Has the intervention in question cooperated with other actors or/and planned their activities in a coherent manner?

*c) Evaluation method:*

Comparative assessment of different peacebuilding actor's strategies, activities and cooperation structures.

*d) Evaluation tools:*

– Internet research
– Survey/group discussion or key stakeholder interviews with relevant peacebuilding actors in the country/area
– Study of documents and interviews with the intervention's staff.

*e) Hints from field experience*

"Everybody wants to coordinate – Nobody wants to be coordinated." This old adage is also very true in the peacebuilding field. From peace research we know that in most cases coherent responses to the challenges of peacebuilding in war-torn societies are much more effective than a single actor's activities. Nevertheless, these findings are not often taken into consideration due to many reasons, including that: international actors often have conflicting interests in a conflict country that hinders coherent approaches; implementing agencies are fighting for the same funding sources and see themselves more as competitors rather than partners, or peacebuilding actors are simply overloaded with too many tasks to think about other actors. We experienced that donor agencies often do have good coordination mechanisms in place, such as the Donor Working Groups on the Peace Process in Sri Lanka, the Donor Peace Support Group in Nepal, or the 'Somalia Aid Coordination Body', which also had subgroups for peacebuilding and governance (see also figure 11). However, this type of coordination does not usually go down to the level of actually coordinating activities on the ground, and strategic coordination for coherent approaches seems difficult. As a result, these forums often serve as vehicles for information exchange rather than for coordination.

We also experienced another phenomenon again and again: when starting new interventions or processes, very little time is invested in finding out what went wrong in the peace process last time and what other actors have already done to address the same problem. The most thrilling negative example comes from the peace process in Somalia, where the intervening international community has mediated or supported a mediation process from 2003-2005 that is very similar to the UN-led peace process in Somalia from 1992-1995. Interestingly enough, all involved actors are not interested in looking back at the failures of the previous processes and applying the lessons learned in the current, ongoing process.

Assessing the actual degree of coherent approach is not very difficult when doing peacebuilding evaluations. We either conducted a mini-survey of other actors' past and present activities in the same field, including an assessment of existing coordination and exchange forums and structures prior to or during the actual evaluation. When we assessed entire country programs, other peace actors were usually very interested in the evaluation and ready to join a workshop or come together for a group meeting. This enabled us to assess the degree of coordination and coherence jointly with the respective actors. It has also proven to be very effective to invite interested actors that run similar programs to the evaluation debriefing workshop, because this can actually facilitate joint future activities.

## 7. Efficiency, Management and Governance

*a) Meaning of the criterion:*

This criterion is used to assess how efficiently the intervention has leveraged its personnel and financial resources as well as how the management and governance system contributed to achieving its outcomes and relationship between inputs and results (see figure 6).

*b) Evaluation questions:*

- Appropriateness of resources spent (financial and human) to reach objectives?
- Could the same results have been achieved with lower costs?
- How efficient is the general management of the intervention (steering, management, organization, structures, governance, processes)?

*c) Evaluation methods:*

- Strength / Weakness Analysis

*d) Evaluation tools:*

- Comparison of project documents, resource spending, budget plan and activities
- Interviews and/or group discussion with staff, partners, and donors
- Check 'do no harm' and gender criteria

*e) Hints from field experience*

Evaluating the efficiency of peacebuilding interventions is just the same as evaluating efficiency for any other type of intervention. However, we found that peace evaluators are not often familiar with evaluating efficiency and thus have a hard time doing so. We therefore recommend that efficiency should be evaluated by somebody on the evaluation team with the respective knowledge.

# 6 Planning Peacebuilding Interventions

In the previous chapter we discussed evaluation in peacebuilding. We have seen that many of the preconditions for evaluation stem from good planning. The objective of this chapter is therefore to share reflections on and give guidelines for planning in peacebuilding with the help of the 'Aid for Peace' framework. This planning process is designed to accommodate the concerns of either policy or program/project peacebuilding interventions.

## What is Planning in Peacebuilding?

Planning in peacebuilding is about identifying the most relevant contribution(s) you or your organization can provide to support peacebuilding in a specific country and design the intervention in such a way that it can reach its objectives effectively. Additionally, proper planning should allow the intervention to be flexible with regard to a possibly-changing environment and to create preconditions for monitoring and evaluation.

Planning in peacebuilding is nothing new: all actors that start peacebuilding interventions plan their interventions. However, contrary to the development field, in peacebuilding we do not have a standardized routine planning instrument like the project cycle management (PCM) with the logical framework approach (see chapter 9). While some peace organizations use strategic-oriented procedures and instruments similar to the PCM, most peacebuilding actors are resistant towards PCM-like approaches because they find them too technical and fear that the essential concept of peacebuilding – the transformation of armed conflicts into peaceful means of resolving disputes and eventually contributing to social change – can simply not be planned in such a systematic way. They further argue that peace processes are too complex and are subject to permanent change, which requires a flexible and open implementation process, one that cannot be planned in detail.

In consequence, most peacebuilding agencies use process-oriented planning based on the findings of peace research. These findings stem from a set of hypotheses that have been developed from peacebuilding theory and lessons learned in peacebuilding (see chapter 4). It is commonly agreed that to achieve sustainable peacebuilding within a society a) certain national actors that can influence the peace process in the short, medium, or long-term need to be supported (for example, civil society groups on the middle or grassroots level of peacebuilding or key actors close to the top leadership level), and b) certain activities need to be implemented to empower these actors (training in conflict resolution skills, dialogue projects, etc.). Because of these hypotheses, many peacebuilding actors assume they already know what or whom to support when they start planning their intervention.

This type of process-oriented planning, however, is confronted with a number of problems. For example, the 'Joint Utstein' study that assessed the peacebuilding efforts of four major donor agencies pointed to the problem that more than 50 percent of the peacebuilding interventions that were analyzed offered no clear analysis of the problem that the intervention sought to address. The study further discovered that most of the assessed interventions lacked a proper intervention strategy as well as a lack of methods and procedures to measure the impact of the interventions on peacebuilding (Smith 2003).

The results of the 'Reflecting on Peace Project' (RPP) that analyzed a broad sample of peacebuilding efforts made by non-governmental organizations were similar. An additional finding of RPP points to the problem that while most peacebuilding interventions make sense within the local context, they often do not effectively link their work to the macro-level context which RPP calls 'peace writ large' (Anderson / Olson 2003).

Most existing planning procedures do not put systematic emphasis on the intervention's impact on the peace process but implicitly assume an automatic cause-effect relationship between the activities of the intervention and the peacebuilding process. This means that they do have an implicit hypothesis of change such as 'peace journalism training leads to more balanced reporting that will influence the conflict parties and the population positively'. It would be better to systematically develop results chains as a sequence of hypotheses of change including indicators that can be monitored throughout the implementation process (see chapter 12).

There is often also a weak understanding of what and how to monitor. Good planning processes should lead the intervention's stakeholders towards an integrated monitoring system. For example, a training and workshop-oriented program traditionally monitors the number of training courses or workshops that have taken place (this, however, is output, see figure 6 and chapter 12) and then assumes that this training will enable the participants to foster changes in the peacebuilding process. However, a good monitoring system continues from here with assessing the outcomes of the training or workshop: Have the participants really used their skills? Were they able to initiate changes in the peacebuilding process? To do such a monitoring, the intervention design needs a clear understanding of what kind of changes should be initiated and how to analyze these changes accordingly. Taking the example of the peace journalism training, the articles, radio or TV news the trained journalists produce after the training need to be analyzed systematically. This task has to be included in the program design from the very beginning. To monitor the impact of this changed reporting on the peace process is a tough task, as it involves finding out whether and how the population and the conflict parties have changed their behavior due to the changed reporting. This could only be assessed at a later stage with in-depth social science research methods such as analysis of public opinion polls.

Information about the situation prior to the start of the intervention is a prerequisite of monitoring, as that allows a before/after comparison (see previous chapter).

Diplomatic peacebuilding actors might think that all the above-mentioned problems mainly related to program and project-oriented interventions. However, good planning is also essential for policy interventions even though the higher an intervention aims, the less frequently we see a proper planning process. There are different reasons for this observation: it has to do with institutional cultures (diplomatic versus project) but also the scope of the intervention and the resources involved. The precondition for a successful mediation or facilitation process is often linked to a certain level of confidentiality that is perceived to be a hindrance to structured planning and especially monitoring procedures. Often, high-level diplomatic policy processes need fewer financial resources than do program interventions, and thus the level of accountability towards the public is perceived to be lower. However, policy interventions can profit as much as any other type of intervention from a good planning and monitoring process.

As a result of all the above-mentioned challenges in peacebuilding planning, it has now become evident that strategically-oriented, systematic planning needs to be combined with process-oriented planning procedures that seek flexible conflict transformation and social change. This can be seen in a number of scholarly publications on the topic in recent years. Fast and Neufeld propose to combine strategic planning with envisioning (Fast / Neufeld 2005), and Rothman provides peacebuilders with a participatory planning and action evaluation approach that also links strategic planning with the envisioning process (Rothman 2003). Paffenholz suggests combining clear goals, strategies, and a context analysis with building a vision for the intervention design (Paffenholz 2001b), while Anderson and Olson propose integrating key elements into the planning process that have proven to be success factors in achieving the micro-macro linkage for effective peacebuilding, the so called RPP-criteria (Anderson / Olson 2003).

In the next part of this chapter we present guidelines for peacebuilding planning that are based on the 'Aid for Peace' framework, which has been enriched by the above mentioned scholarly findings, and our own field testing.

## Guidelines for a Good Planning Process

The 'Aid for Peace' framework can be used as a planning matrix for peacebuilding interventions on the program as well as on the policy level. In applying systematically the four parts of the framework (see chapter 2), the user will end up with an intervention plan with a) goals that address the peacebuilding needs in the country, b) a focus on the comparative advantages of the involved actors, c) assurance that the intervention incorporates potential negative effects into the implementation design and d) hypotheses developed for possible positive effects (outcomes and impacts) of the intervention that are incorporated into a monitoring system, and e) understanding of when in the planning process to best make use of which kinds of tools (like the RPP-criteria).

As the general functioning of the 'Aid for Peace' framework has been already described in chapter 2, we will now focus on the process that needs to be conducted when applying the framework to planning peacebuilding interventions.

The main planning process happens during a participatory stakeholder workshop that needs to be prepared as part of a conflict and peace processes analysis and – pending the status of intervention planning – also during a peacebuilding baseline study. In case the general direction of an intervention is still unclear, the baseline study will be conducted only after the workshop. As a result of the workshop, the intervention design can be written down (project/ program proposal or policy strategy) and a monitoring system needs to be established. Good peacebuilding planning is comprised out of the following steps:

1. Decision/brainstorming about the possible intervention
2. Taking stock and assessing the status of available information
3. Data collection, which includes conducting or commissioning conflict/peace analysis studies, collecting information about other actor's interventions and conducting a peacebuilding baseline study (if already possible)
4. Selection of stakeholders and preparing the workshop
5. Conducting the workshop which implies discussing or analyzing the intervention's context, conducting a Peacebuilding Relevance Assessment, setting intervention priorities, anticipating and discussing risks, anticipating effects with the help of developing results chains and monitoring indicators and finally developing an action plan
6. Conducting/Commissioning the peacebuilding baseline study (if not done earlier)
7. Writing the intervention design

In the following text we describe each individual step of the planning process in more detail.

## 1. Decision/brainstorming about the possible intervention

At the beginning of a planning process there is a reason for a possible intervention. Actors in peacebuilding aim to contribute to a particular peace process for a variety of reasons: because they are national organizations from within a country at conflict and want to contribute to transforming the armed conflict into peaceful means of managing differences; they wish to contribute to preventing an outbreak of armed conflict, or they support post-conflict peacebuilding. External actors in peacebuilding are either requested by internal actors to support their peacebuilding efforts or decide on their own to support peacebuilding in that particular country. Pending who you are as an organization, your contribution with regard to roles and functions, influence, level of peacebuilding addressed and timeframe considered can vary greatly and requires different intervention strategies. The objective of a planning process is to find out how your organization can best contribute to peacebuilding in the particular context.

Often there are two different stages involved in beginning a planning process: either an actor or an organization is still in the brainstorming phase and will start a planning process from the very beginning, or an actor/organization already has an idea of its comparative advantage and wants to analyze whether and how these functions can be applied in the specific conflict context. For example, peacebuilding organizations that are specialized in conflict resolution training and dialogue workshops know that this is what they can offer for peacebuilding. They need to find out with the help of the planning process, what kind of training or dialogue is needed in the particular conflict in question, what are the possible partners and stakeholders and how to proceed in order to contribute to positive changes in the peace process.

In this step it is therefore important to determine the starting point for a planning process.

## 2. Taking stock and assessing the status of available information

When this decision is taken, we need to find out what information is needed for the planning process and subsequently determine what of that is already available and what needs to be collected. In general we need:

An analysis of the peacebuilding needs in the country. To obtain the needed information we need a) an analysis of the armed conflict and the status of the peace process in the country and/or in a particular region or area of potential intervention (see chapter 1 and chapter 12); b) an analysis of different future developments of the conflict and peace environment in order to plan for a flexible intervention design; and c) a clear vision for peace in the country at question on which the intervention is based.

The involved stakeholders might want to develop or analyze this vision jointly in the planning workshop. In this case, you need to analyze prior to the workshop the main different peace visions of the involved stakeholders in the country – if they have any. For example, in Sri Lanka the conflict parties have different visions of how a peaceful Sri Lanka would look. While the LTTE envisions an island divided into two states or at least two separate entities where the LTTE controlled areas would have a status of high regional autonomy, the government of Sri Lanka sees a one-state solution where the problem of armed conflict is in the past. What this one-state solution should look like, as well as the extent of regional autonomy or minority rights for the Tamil population, remains unclear as different members of the political elite have different opinions. The international community has yet another vision for a peaceful Sri Lanka, a one-state solution with a decentralized system of governance and minority rights. When planning an intervention in such a situation, it is important to find out your own vision for peace and make it transparent to your intervention's stakeholders or else develop a joint vision.

Moreover, you need d) a list of short-, medium-, and long-term needs for peacebuilding in the country. On the basis of this list, priorities for the intervention's goals and activities will be defined; you might want to develop or analyze these needs jointly in the planning workshop. In this case you analyze the conflict and peacebuilding context and collect the necessary information for the joint development of the peacebuilding needs.

We also need information on what other actors that are involved in peacebuilding in the same country or region have already done and are doing. This enables us to adapt the intervention strategy accordingly and avoid doing the same things others are already doing or else avoid the same mistakes others have made in the past.

In case we already know what type of intervention we are planning to support (due to comparative institutional advantages or previous experience the same context), we need also to know in more detail if and how the envisaged goals and activities will fit into the particular context in order to contribute to peacebuilding. For this purpose a peacebuilding baseline study needs to be conducted.

We want to know what kind of potential risks the intervention might face when pursued in the envisaged direction. Whether such a risk assessment will be done prior, during or after a planning workshop depends greatly on the specific intervention context (see risk assessment checklist in chapter 12). For example, if you are an international NGO from a country that has bad relationships with one of the conflict parties, you need to analyze prior to a possible engagement whether you would be accepted as an outsider in this context. Or, if you are an external religiously-based organization that usually supports local religious groups in their peacebuilding efforts, you need to find out the status and role of these groups within the conflict setting.

## 3. Data collection

Pending the outcome of the stock-taking exercise, studies or surveys need to be conducted or commissioned. It is also important to find out whether such studies need to be done in the field or whether sufficient information is already available to analyze the situation in a systematic way.

Furthermore, it is necessary to have a clear idea about the available financial and human resources necessary for conducting the studies and decide accordingly to involve somebody from the organization, local partners, researchers or else commission the study to external researcher/consultants (see chapter 12 for hints).

## 4. Selection of stakeholders and preparing the workshop

When the results of the studies are available, the participatory planning workshop needs to be prepared. In order to do this we need to have clarity about the objectives of the workshop, the stakeholders to be involved, the time and funds available, the need for an external or internal facilitator, the planning methods, tools and processes used within the four parts of the 'Aid for Peace' framework, and the venue of the workshop (headquarters or field).

Answers to these questions depend on the specific planning process, the organizational culture, resources, timing, and scope of the planned intervention. For example, for a short term policy intervention that aims at finding out short-term measures to support the negotiation teams of the conflict parties with expertise, most of the information should come from the pre-studies and the planning workshop itself might only last two hours or half a day, whereas an organization that plans to get involved in a country for a longer period of time should have a planning workshop that reflects this duration and intensity.

The selection process for the participants of the workshop is key to its success. For program/project interventions, the relevant staff from headquarters and the field should participate as well as local partners (if already identified). In case the intervention context is not fully clear it can also be helpful to invite local and/ or external experts to the first part of the workshop where the context is being analyzed.

For policy interventions, especially more diplomatic ones that require a certain degree of confidentiality, it is advisable to invite external resource persons into the workshop in order to profit from their knowledge. There are two ways to cope with the issue of confidentiality: a) the experts only remain during the first part of the workshop where the intervention context is discussed or b) the experts sign a confidentiality clause. The advantage of this latter approach is that the same experts can be used as a reference group for monitoring and advising the intervention's implementation. For example, the Swedish Life and Peace Institute (LPI) has worked jointly with the UN in Somalia from 1992 to 1995. LPI set up a Reference Group that gave advice to the UN throughout the process. The idea of a Reference Group was later taken up by the Head of the UN Lessons Learned Unit within the UN Department of Peacekeeping Operations, who was involved in Somalia (Paffenholz 2003).

Professional facilitation is needed for the workshop. Whether an external or internal facilitator is required depends on the organization's resources and culture (for skills and knowledge see chapter 12).

### 5. Conducting the workshop

In the course of the workshop we aim to complete such tasks as: discussing or analyzing the intervention's context; conducting a Peacebuilding Relevance Assessment; setting intervention priorities; anticipating and discussing risks; anticipating effects through developing results chains; establishing monitoring indicators, and developing an action plan.

How these objectives are achieved depends on the specific workshop and the methodologies the facilitator has chosen or agreed upon with the stakeholders.

*Discussing or analyzing the intervention's context*

In the first part of the workshop, the peacebuilding needs should be either discussed or analyzed jointly (see chapter 2 and hints in chapter 12). Depending on the specific workshop design and knowledge of the intervention's stakeholders, the analysis of the peacebuilding needs will be done jointly or the results of the pre-study will be presented and discussed with the stakeholders (and the invited experts). First, the analysis of the conflict and peacebuilding context is begun, followed by the peacebuilding deficiency analysis. The peacebuilding needs analysis is based on the vision for peacebuilding in the country and tries to identify the deficiencies and the missing needs that keep that vision from being realized. There are different possibilities for how to reach for such a vision (see chapter 2). Once the peacebuilding needs are identified, they are compared with the conflict and peace analysis. During the workshop we have had good experience with visualizing the needs for peacebuilding on a bulletin board or wall and clustering them into short-, medium- and long-term needs. In such a way it is easier to decide which needs the intervention wants to address.

*Conducting a Peacebuilding Relevance Assessment:*
*Setting intervention priorities*

The objective of the peacebuilding relevance assessment is to compare the needs for peacebuilding with the organization's comparative advantages, mission statement, goals, and resources as well as to consider other actors' interventions (see relevance scale in chapter 12).

Another workshop practice we have found successful in this stage is to write other actors' interventions on cards and pin them next to the peacebuilding need they seek to address. In addition, participants list their own intervention's comparative advantages on a separate pin board or flipchart. This quickly enables the workshop participants to judge what kinds of peacebuilding needs can be best addressed by the organization.

In a next step the needs to be addressed can be formulated into objectives and activities can be also discussed. In case insufficient information is available on activities, this is subject to the peacebuilding baseline study after the workshop. The baseline study could be included in the planning process as the first implementation step. For example, a program that identified broad-based participation in the peace process as the main peacebuilding need they wanted to address held long debates in the workshop that ended with the conclusion to support civil society movements and networks. However, the information on the structure and composition of the different groups was missing, which hindered the creation of a proper program design. Therefore a baseline study had to be conducted before they could proceed with the planning process. In another workshop the intervening organization had decided prior to the workshop that it was going to support women's participation in peacebuilding and had commissioned a baseline study prior to the workshop. With the available information on the status of women in society, gender relations within the peace process, and the status and composition of women's groups in the country, it was possible to decide exactly what kinds of needs could be addressed with the help of what kinds of partners and activities.

At this stage of planning, the RPP-criteria can be also used for cross-checking whether the now planned goals and activities will contribute to effective peacebuilding (see http://www.cdainc.com).

*Anticipating and discussing risks*

By this point in the planning process the intervention's goals and general activities have been identified. Now we want to explore what kinds of risks the planned intervention could encounter when starting implementation, and what could be done to reduce these risks. In case the risk assessment has already been part of the pre-study, the results are being presented and discussed in the workshop or else the risk assessment will be conducted now with the help of a risk assessment questionnaire (see chapter 2). For example, in the case of the above-mentioned intervention aiming at enhancing women's participation in peacebuilding, the risks assessment pointed to the fact that a women's NGO was monopolizing the process because they were equally well-connected to one of the conflict parties and to the donor community. During the workshop it was discussed how to deal with this issue and a strategy was designed to cooperate with the group and at the same time reduce their influence.

Anticipating effects with the help of developing results chains, monitoring indicators and 'Do no Harm' check

At this stage of the workshop results chains and indicators will be jointly developed for all the main planned activity lines as a means of making the hypotheses of change operational and also in order to be able to later monitor and evaluate the achievements of the interventions (please refer to chapter 2 and figure 6). We want to create a causal linkage between the peacebuilding needs we wish to address through our intervention (our objectives) and the activities planned. In other words, we want to find out whether the activities planned are the correct ones for reaching the peacebuilding need and hence lead to our desired change within the peace process.

Monitoring indicators that will also be developed help to identify additional activities that might be needed for monitoring purposes. For example, when conducting training or dialogue workshops, it is necessary to come up with an impact hypothesis, e.g. a results chain on what changes we expect to achieve through training these groups of people, and how we intend to monitor the changes. Usually peacebuilding interveners do not properly monitor the changes but rely on an implicit assumption that the intended change will occur automatically. In order to avoid such guess work, we need to define monitoring indicators. For example, to monitor the outputs of such training, the program reports will give sufficient information on how many courses have been held. To monitor outcomes, we want to know how to find indicators that help us to monitor the changes made by the participants within the peace process. Here we probably need to include additional activities in the program that enable us to analyze the participants' actions initiated after the workshops (see also the example of the journalist training). In order to monitor the impact of the training on the macro-level peace process (the micro-macro linkage), we need to plan for a survey or assessment at a later stage, for example towards the end of the intervention (see example of LPI trainees in the peace process in chapter 5). During the workshop it is important to gain clarity about the possible indicators that can be useful and whether additional program activities are required due to the monitoring.

It is also important to anticipate potential negative effects of the intervention. It is helpful to do a 'Do no Harm' check at this stage (see http://www.cdainc.com).

*Developing an action plan*

Finally, the results of the workshop will be summarized in an action plan that also includes responsibilities and follow-up steps. An important part of the action plan is to adapt the planned intervention strategy to the different conflict scenarios as developed earlier. In practice this involves a discussion of the validity of the intervention strategy and each planned activity line in light of the different scenarios. As a result of these discussions, the implementation plan will be adapted accordingly or slightly different implementation plans need to be designed for different scenarios. This is an essential step since the situation in conflict zones is subject to rapid change. For example, an intervention that had been designed in Nepal during the peace negotiations aimed at supporting broad-based participation in the peace process. For the negotiation scenario, a set of activities were planned to support discussion forums for civil society groups that were aimed at discussing the same issues being discussed at the negotiation table. It was planned that the results of the civil society discussions would be communicated to the negotiation parties. For the scenario of a break down of the negotiation process, it was planned to support networking of civil society groups in combination with capacity building to prepare civil society for a role within a future negotiation process.

One critical component of the action plan which should not be overlooked is the decision on the next implementation steps, whether it should be conducting a peacebuilding baseline study or writing a program proposal or policy intervention plan.

Looking at the described planning process with the 'Aid for Peace' framework we have seen that combining a systematic, analysis-based strategic planning with a process- and vision-oriented approach will create good conditions for effective peacebuilding. This combination works by articulating clear and measurable goals that can hold peacebuilders accountable and responsible while still allowing adequate flexibility for reaching a successful conflict transformation process that contributes to sustainable social change.

# Part III

# Planning and Evaluating Development
# and
# Humanitarian Interventions in Conflict Zones

# 7    Understanding Peace and Conflict Sensitive Development and Humanitarian Action

## What is Peace and Conflict Sensitivity and Why is it Needed?

Today the topic of peace and conflict sensitivity has successfully entered the agenda of development donors and agencies and is also widely accepted within the field of humanitarian action; we have seen a tremendous institutionalization and conceptualization of the topic in recent years. Most donor and larger development agencies nowadays have a unit or an advisor for conflict and peace under different headings. Almost all organizations have a developed strategy for peace and conflict sensitive development or humanitarian action, mostly based on the OECD guidelines for conflict, peace, and development (OECD 2001).

Despite the series of recent international changes, dealing with peace and conflict was nothing new; from ancient times different actors have made contributions to peacebuilding. However, only after the end of the Cold War in the beginning of the 1990s, the international community was increasingly confronted with a series of internal wars for which the international legal framework was not sufficiently prepared. With the 'Agenda for Peace' (Boutros-Ghali 1992) the international community began to wrestle with adjusting international mechanisms to better deal with such conflicts; this process, taken a step further by the reports of the UN Secretary-General on preventing armed conflict (Annan 2002) and security, development and human rights (Annan 2005) a decade later still continues (see chapter 4).

We are referring to this process when we talk about 'peace and conflict sensitivity' in this book; specifically, we mean integrating the peace and conflict lens into development and humanitarian policies and programs. We sometimes also simply use the term 'aid' for describing both development and humanitarian action. By applying a peace/conflict sensitive lens, aid donors and agencies want to reduce the risk that aid could inadvertently escalate conflict; first by 'doing no harm' and secondly by contributing directly or indirectly to peacebuilding.

It is, however, important to understand the difference between peacebuilding interventions as discussed in Part II of this book and the contribution of development and humanitarian action to peacebuilding. While peacebuilding interventions directly aim at building peace, development and humanitarian action have other objectives, be it poverty reduction or reducing human suffering. Despite this difference, development and humanitarian action can both reduce unintended negative effects on armed conflict and contribute to peacebuilding in various ways through peace and conflict sensitive development policies and programs or through humanitarian action.

Why is peace and conflict sensitivity in development and humanitarian action needed? There are five primary reasons why a peace/conflict lens should be applied to development and humanitarian work, which we list in more detail below.

### Working in conflict zones can put development policies and programs at risk

All development interventions taking place in situations of latent or manifest armed conflict or in the aftermath of war or destructive conflict have a much higher risk of failing than do interventions in 'normal' situations. Often interventions face problems such as security risks for program staff and infrastructure, lack of access to beneficiaries and program partners, or a political climate that hinders work in conflict-affected areas or with all relevant actors. When working in conflict zones, therefore, development and humanitarian organizations have to be well prepared for such obstacles and all possible risks should be built into intervention designs.

### Well-intentioned development interventions can do harm

The many well-intentioned aid efforts undertaken by the international community have not always been fully effective, and sometimes they have even had negative effects on the potential and actual level of violence. For example, many development projects in Sri Lanka and Nepal were recruiting local staff solely on the basis of qualifications, thereby disregarding the ethnic, religious or caste composition of their staff and thus supporting only groups from one conflict party or from dominant groups. Aid agencies in Somalia paid militia groups to transport food to the hungry and thereby provided warlords with moral and material support to run their war enterprises.

### Almost all interventions can contribute also to peacebuilding

Peace-oriented interventions are explicitly intended to contribute to peacebuilding directly. However, since the 'Do no Harm' debate, we know that other interventions can also contribute directly or indirectly to peacebuilding, assuming that they are aware of this potential. This does not mean that all intervention designs have to be completely changed: a development program must concern itself first of all with its contribution to development. However, by applying a peace and conflict sensitive approach to development, actors can systematically find out whether and how it is possible to contribute to peacebuilding in addition to their primary objective. Such programming sensitivity is becoming increasingly more necessary, as sustainable social and economic development is impossible without peace.

### Peace and conflict are highly political issues

When working in conflict zones, development actors are faced with a variety of very political challenges. Traditionally, for most governmental donors and agencies, the government of a country is the main partner for development. When working in conflict zones, however, this partner is also a conflict party, which often makes traditional cooperation difficult. This challenge is further compounded in conflict areas because agencies are confronted with the problem of dealing with armed non-state groups that are opposing the government partner. These groups may directly challenge programs sponsored by the government, or may pose a safety threat to aid workers trying to access regions where such groups are in control. This leads to another challenge, which is the need for development programs, and even more for humanitarian work, to reach out to the affected population; often remote areas are most prone to control by anti-government groups. In response to these challenges, aid actors have to engage in much more effective coordination efforts within the aid community as well as with foreign policy makers. This cooperation is often challenged by different political interests within the donor community, often manifested in conflicting positions around the "war on terrorism" (e.g. military versus non-military solutions to armed conflicts).

*Standard planning and evaluation methods need to be adapted to the conflict situation*

When planning or evaluating an intervention in a conflict zone, one can make use of traditional planning and assessment methods and tools as provided by the development and humanitarian community or by research on policy evaluation. Many development organizations argue that their planning and assessment methods and tools are internationally accepted; that the logic of planning and evaluation is the same in conflict and non-conflict zones; and that consequentially there is no need to adapt them to conflict situations. However, we frequently hear reservations against the use and adaptation of these traditional methods and tools from peacebuilding organizations, which argue that armed conflict and peacebuilding are such complex phenomena that these standard methods are not appropriate for planning and evaluating peacebuilding interventions.

In taking a closer look at internationally agreed planning procedures and evaluation criteria for development interventions (see weblinks in chapter 12), we see that neither argument is either totally right or totally wrong. In fact, many of the standard criteria for planning and evaluating development or humanitarian work are fully applicable to work within conflict zones, though others need to be adapted or augmented because conflict situations are more complex. The 'Aid for Peace' approach takes these findings into consideration, builds upon existing knowledge, but takes it a step further by adding new dimensions of analysis and by integrating different levels of intervention.

## The Nexus between Conflict/Peace and Development/Humanitarian Action: A Short History

Development cooperation and humanitarian action have always had a self-understanding of being less political than other international actors. As already mentioned in chapter 1, this view was challenged with the tragic events around the 1994 genocide in Rwanda, where the genocide took development actors by surprise. In the aftermath of the Rwandan crisis, a major debate started among development actors about the role of development in conflict affected areas. This first debate was characterized by two discussions:

The first discussion centered on the possibilities for preventing another situation like the one in Rwanda from happening. This was the beginning of the interest in political early warning, a topic that has since been absorbed into the general debate about prevention (see chapter 4).

The second discussion emerged from research conducted in the aftermath of Rwanda (Uvin 1998) and in other conflict affected countries (Anderson 1999). The results clearly demonstrated that aid can do harm in conflict situations and that, inadvertently, it has negative effects on conflict dynamics. Further research explored assessment methods and tools for responding to these findings in a constructive way: From 1996 onwards, Mary B. Anderson and her team developed the 'Local Capacities for Peace Approach' (better known as 'Do no Harm') with a planning matrix and checklists for finding out the potential effects of aid projects on conflict and peace. The 'Do no Harm' debate is a major success story in the peace and development fields: it has developed almost into a "mantra" of a new understanding of aid work in conflict zones.

In the same vein, Luc Reychler and his colleagues started developing 'Conflict Impact Assessment Systems' (CIAS) focusing on macro-level policy from 1996 onwards (Reychler 1999), while Kenneth Bush developed a 'Peace and Conflict Impact Assessment' (PCIA) methodology comparable to environmental or gender impact assessments; like these other assessment tools, PCIA was also designed for project level interventions (Bush 1998).

Kenneth Bush's research triggered an intensive debate about PCIA possibilities and limitations (Bush 1998, Leonhardt 2002, Berghof Handbook 2002 and 2005). Both 'Do no Harm' and PCIA originally focused mainly on international or local NGO aid projects, but their popularity quickly spread and they were used by a variety of other organizations as well. Large international NGOs and a number of donor agencies have adapted the 'Do no Harm' approach to fit within their organizational operational procedures and apply it in the field through training of staff and partners. Good examples are the systematic incorporation of the 'Do no Harm' approach into the work of CARE International and a variety of European NGOs such as World Vision or the German Protestant Development Service.

Interestingly, the development community is much more concerned with the peace and conflict sensitivity debate then the humanitarian community. The humanitarian community has partly reflected the 'Do no Harm' discussion but has not engaged in a general debate about peace and conflict sensitivity on a broad scale. The reason stems from the fact that humanitarian actors are more familiar with working in conflict situations. For most of them the practical implications of the 'Do no Harm' debate are interesting, however humanitarian actors find it also difficult to incorporate a conflict lens as they think of themselves of being apolitical. Moreover, it has been also difficult to break the cycle of routine in humanitarian action that has to deliver quickly. On the other hand, development actors were not used to working in conditions of armed conflict, because when an armed conflict started, development workers tended to hand their work over to the humanitarian field. This practice has changed in the last decade due the nature of armed intra-state conflict: More and more traditional development countries have slowly slid into armed conflict. Today development work is often possible in some parts of a country, while other areas are heavily affected by armed conflict. For example in Southern Uganda, Northern Sudan or Southern Sri Lanka traditional development work is/was going on, while in the other parts of the countries a war is/was going on. Today we rarely see armed conflicts on a large scale affecting the entire territory of a country. Thus, development actors remain while humanitarian actors only work in some parts of the country. Moreover, admitting that a country is suffering from armed conflict is already a political statement that is often avoided by development actors and their partner governments.

In addition to the above-mentioned changes, nowadays development actors enter the post-conflict reconstruction scene much earlier and apply reconstruction or emergency oriented development approaches more frequently.

As armed conflicts are subject to rapid change, development actors are engaged in constant discussions about the possibilities of continuing or ending development work or finding different aid delivery modes. All these circumstances challenge the traditional way of doing development work. Thus, donors and agencies are looking for ways and means to cope with these challenges.

Currently, discussions move into the following different directions:

First, many organizations now use the term peace and conflict-sensitive development or similar terms (De la Haye / Denayer 2003, Paffenholz 2005d) which is understood as an overall term to describe different efforts, methods and tools for working in conflict zones with the objective to, at least, avoid doing harm and, if possible, also contribute positively to peacebuilding. In our book we use the term 'Peace and Conflict Sensitive Development' in order to make clear that we are not only talking about reducing conflict and avoiding harm, but also about contributing to peacebuilding.

The term PCIA or often just PCA (Peace and Conflict Assessment) (BMZ 2005) still prevails but is used more to describe assessment procedures, methods and tools, while peace and conflict sensitivity as such is broader and used as an overarching term.

Second, the integration of the peace and conflict lens has reached the organizational, managerial level and thus goes beyond program implementation. This stems from understanding and experience that successful mainstreaming requires a lot of organizational and management changes by the organizations involved (see chapter 11). A main obstacle derives from the fact that the expert community still falls short of providing sufficient capacity to support these peace/conflict mainstreaming processes, especially on the local field level. Many governmental agencies are putting more emphasis on training their staff and assigning conflict or peacebuilding advisors to the field offices in order to ensure operational peace and conflict mainstreaming. The UNDP's Bureau of Crisis Prevention and Recovery, like many other multi- and bi-lateral donors and agencies have seconded a number of these advisors to their field offices, while NGOs opt for building local capacities through training. In addition, we find nowadays several different types of peace/conflict advisors. The conflict advisors from the Ministries of Development Cooperation from Britain (DfID) or Sweden (SIDA), for example, are working on the political level, whereas the peace/conflict advisors of the German Technical Cooperation (GTZ) are working on the operational mainstreaming level; the UNDP peace/conflict advisors usually work on both levels.

Third, the development community is also engaged in a debate on how to cope with so-called fragile contexts. As many fragile contexts are also conflict countries, we see more and more of a linkage between these two debates as the development community continues to wrestle with the issue of aid effectiveness. Development actors are increasingly coming to the conclusion that aid is only effective when recipient countries adopt sound policies and nurture effective institutions. The problem with this finding, however, is how to deal with so-called poor performing countries that are mostly countries in fragile contexts; many are often also countries with ongoing armed conflicts or find themselves in the aftermath of wars or armed conflict. It has been acknowledged that special attention needs to be given to those countries (Paris High-Level Forum 2005), while keeping in mind that currently almost 50% of all international cooperation countries find themselves in fragile contexts. So far the donor community has dealt with the problem of fragile states by 'staying engaged' and seeking the best ways of continued aid delivery so that people are not be held responsible for the poor performance of their leaders (Centre for the Future State 2005; Debiel / Terlinden 2005; Leader 2005; OECD 2005 a and b); Paffenholz 2006; Rosser et al. 2006).

Fourth, donors, researchers, and implementing agencies have started to reflect on the effectiveness and impact of peacebuilding interventions. This triggered a new wave of publications and conferences on how to evaluate peacebuilding interventions (see more in chapters 4 and 5). This has also shifted the debate towards the direction of peace organizations and away from development per se. This debate is sometimes also referred to under the label of 'conflict sensitivity' (Resource Pack 2004); however, the essence of the debate is about professionalizing planning and evaluation procedures within the peace community and not about introducing a new concept (see part II of this book). We therefore only talk about development and humanitarian work when we refer to peace and conflict sensitivity.

## What does the Practice of Peace and Conflict Sensitive Work look like?

Development and humanitarian action can actually contribute to peacebuilding in different ways on different levels:

1) On the macro political level through targeted policy interventions such as conditionality of aid resources, negotiated benchmarks, identifying humanitarian entry points for peace negotiations, or international measures against war economy (Paffenholz 2005d): here we see a close overlap with traditional diplomacy, thus these interventions require close cooperation between development and foreign policy actors.
2) On the development sector level through inculcating conflict and peace issues into development sector strategies.
3) On the operational level (programs and projects) through:
   – the way traditional aid programs and projects work in conflict environments, nowadays referred to under the label of 'peace and conflict sensitive development' (Paffenholz 2005d) or 'Do no Harm' (Anderson 1999);
   – support to new types of programs and projects that are directly related to the objective 'peacebuilding,' such as support for capacity building or training for local peace organizations and networks, peace journalism training, demining, or demobilization activities. Development donors and agencies today fund or implement a wide variety of projects/initiatives. In this section, however, we do not discuss these types of interventions as the same rules apply for them as for the traditional peacebuilding interventions covered in Part II of the book.

In the text that follows we take a closer look into the various contributions to peacebuilding made by development or humanitarian action.

## The political level

As mentioned above, in addition to diplomatic peacebuilding efforts such as mediation or good offices (Paffenholz 2001a), bi- and multi-lateral donors can apply different policy-oriented strategies such as conditionality, negotiated benchmarks, bottom lines, or policy dialogue. In addition, donors can establish international networks against war economies by linking aid to conflict and peacebuilding in order to influence the conflict parties (Paffenholz 2005d , Uvin 1999, OECD 2001, Wood 2003). Here, we wish to go into more detail regarding each of these strategies and their implications for development and humanitarian actors.

*Conditionality* implies defining certain conditions under which aid will be provided. The objective of these conditions is to influence the conflict situation in a positive way, e.g. stopping a major actor from continuing armed conflict or gross human rights violations by reducing or stopping aid resources and linking their restart to certain political conditions. For example, in December 2005 major donors such as the European Union and the World Bank stopped budgetary support to Ethiopia because the government had committed human rights violations against political opposition. The same happened in the aftermath of the so-called 'Royal Coup' in Nepal in February 2005, when the Nepali King dissolved parliament and jailed political leaders, human rights activists and journalists.

*Negotiated benchmarks* are the opposite side of conditionality, using a positive incentive, e.g. more aid will be provided if certain conditions in the country improve.

*Bottom lines* define the end of donor engagement, i.e. 'if the situation doesn't improve, we will stop our engagement with the country'. Usually the concrete issues that need to be improved for example, end of undemocratic move of the Nepali King, will be announced as well as a time frame.

*Policy dialogue* is long-term engagement, usually with a cooperative partner government. Donors hope to be able to influence policies in a constructive direction through their long-term relationship with a partner country

*Identifying entry points for peace negotiations* is a traditional mediation/facilitation intervention that is usually performed by diplomatic actors or NGOs. However, we have seen successful cases where entry points for peace negotiations have been created during war times with the help of humanitarian action. For example, during the war in El Salvador, the humanitarian church agencies negotiated short ceasefires in order to proceed with child vaccination. Towards the end of the Mozambique war, the International Committee of the Red Cross negotiated humanitarian corridors where the conflicting parties were not allowed to enter and humanitarian aid could be delivered. Both interventions had a tremendous effect on speeding up the peace process. In El Salvador, people started pressuring for peace after seeing that the conflict parties were able to agree to a ceasefire. In Mozambique, the humanitarian corridors had the effect of more and more people leaving the war zones, which put pressure on one conflict party and speeded up their willingness to negotiate.

*International networks against war economies,* like the fairly successful Kimberly process for banning war diamonds, involves trying to eliminate the resource base from the conflicting parties through control of the markets. Other current processes, such as efforts to make oil revenue in conflict affected countries transparent, or attempts to create alternatives to the drug trade in Afghanistan or Colombia, have so far not proven to be effective.

All (except for the last) of these policy measures build on the hypothesis that aid in combination with international reputation is an attractive and valued resource for conflicting parties. Thus, most of these measures can only have an effect on the situation if a country is donor dependent and does not wish to lose these resources. For example, oil-exporting Angola, which does not rely on foreign aid, has been more or less resistant to donor pressure.

The policy level of development has also become very difficult as it challenges donor/partner relations. Here donors are faced with a number of critical questions/ issues, such as their relationship to the government, one of the conflict parties; the difficult engagement with 'armed non-state actors', and the linkages between diplomatic and development actors.

A study of the work of the Swiss Development Cooperation in Nepal during the armed conflict shows that there is a need to link the political with the operational level (Paffenholz 2006).

## The operational level

It is now commonly accepted in the development practitioner/expert community that on the operational level development actors have three choices when working in conflict zones (Goodhand 2001):

– Working *around* conflict: Conflict is seen as a negative risk factor that is to be avoided;
– Working *in* conflict: Actors have a certain awareness that development can influence conflict and try to avoid negative effects on the conflict situation (Do no Harm);
– Working *on* conflict: Actors are also aware that all development work can contribute to peacebuilding. They apply peace and conflict sensitive approaches to development, which also includes proactive peacebuilding work.

The overall objective of all strategies and approaches is the same, i.e. designing development and humanitarian policies and programs in order to ensure that aid is not inadvertently doing harm and that its peacebuilding potential is directed towards working *in* and *on* conflict.

Peace and conflict sensitive approaches and analytical tools for supporting development and humanitarian work in and on conflict are mainly inspired by peace research and participatory development. Today we find these approaches grouped under different labels such as 'peace/conflict sensitivity,' 'Do no Harm,' or 'Peace and Conflict (Impact) Assessment' (PC[I]A). The only common denominator between these approaches and methodologies is the need to conduct a conflict analysis; consequently, many tools for conflict analysis are available (Resource Pack

2004 and chapter 12). This similarity aside, all existing approaches explored thus far differ on a variety of characteristics, most notably with regard to the type(s) of intervention(s) (development or peace) and actors (peace/aid, donors/NGOs) they are designed for; the level of intervention (policy, program/project) they target; the level of linkage between the conflict/peace analysis and the intervention design; the comprehensiveness and clarity of methods and tools provided; and the values, norms and research assumptions on which the approaches are based.

In practice, peace and conflict sensitivity on the ground often boils down to finding answers to the following crucial questions (the four **W**s):

1.  **What** is our work?
    Are the issues addressed by the intervention still relevant in light of the conflict situation and can they also address peacebuilding in the country?

2.  With **Whom** do we work?
    Has the intervention involved all conflict and peace relevant actors when it comes to staff recruitment and selection of stakeholders (beneficiaries and partners)?

3.  **Where** do we work?
    Has the intervention reflected all the respective geographical areas in the country that need to be supported in light of the conflict analysis and the needs for peacebuilding in the country? (This does not mean that a program has to work everywhere, but it should be aware of where it works and what the effects of this decision can be on peace and conflict).

4.  In which **Way** do we work?
    Is the intervention planning and implementation organized in a peace and conflict sensitive way that reflects participation of all relevant actors, promotes gender balance, and supports local actors to build long-term structures for peacebuilding?

## Conclusions and Challenges

This chapter has given an overview of the topic of 'peace and conflict sensitivity' in development and humanitarian action. We have seen that the incorporation of a peace/conflict lens into development and humanitarian work started only after the tragic event of Rwanda in 1994. At the same time, the peacebuilding field started to mature and is currently engaged in a debate about professionalization (see part II of this book). Today the peace and conflict topic is one of the most successful mainstreaming topics on the development agenda.

After Rwanda the topic of peace and conflict sensitivity was discussed as a very political issue and has since then shifted into a tool-based discussion. In the past few years a variety of tool-based approaches have been developed. The availability of so many approaches has, unfortunately, watered down the concept of peace/conflict sensitivity and PCIA and contributed to a great deal of confusion among development and humanitarian actors. However, only a few approaches are comprehensive and also useful for a variety of different actors on all levels of interventions. Important requirements for evaluating good approaches are a) the systematic link between the analysis of the conflict and peacebuilding environment with the implementation of interventions in conflict zones in a systematic step-by-step process, b) the merger between a theory of social change and conflict transformation with professional, operational requirements for policy and program planning and implementation.

For a long time the discussion has focused on development and to a lesser extent on humanitarian action and it has only recently shifted towards the professionalization of the peacebuilding field. Although at first it seemed the field of development could learn a lot from the peacebuilding field; it seems that the field of peacebuilding could also learn from the planning and evaluation processes in development. Despite the progress that has been made, a number of challenges for peace and conflict sensitivity in development and humanitarian action are still ahead:

*Re-politicization needed*

There is a need to re-politicize the debate around peace/conflict sensitivity (Bush 2005a and b, Paffenholz 2005b and c). Often the available policy concepts are not sufficiently applied as donors find it hard to reach for coherent policies in conflict-affected countries. However, peace and conflict are political issues and foster the need for better cooperation between diplomatic, development and humanitarian actors.

The overwhelming aid donations to Tsunami affected Sri Lanka have also created a set of severe problems around political peace and conflict insensitivity. The first problem is linked to the amount of aid: the donor post-Tsunami needs assessment came to the conclusion that there are four to five times more aid resources in the country than needed (see: http://www.tsunami-evaluation.org). This led to over-funding in a lot of sectors, thereby favoring certain groups over others. Second, the over-funding shifted the power balance in the conflict setting towards the government, which consequently did not need to make any compromises towards the other conflict party, the LTTE. As an effect, we saw increased political tensions and violence in the country. Third, the many private aid organizations especially founded for the Tsunami aid delivery, had no experiences in development or humanitarian action in general and thus also no idea about peace and conflict sensitivity. This compounded the problems of unjust resource distribution. Fourth, the large amount of aid resources that needed to be spent quickly created a need to work mainly with the government given its quick absorption capacities. This fuelled one of the root causes of conflict, e.g. the unjust regional distribution of resources. In consequence, the LTTE-controlled areas in the North and East got far less Tsunami aid than the South, because there agencies had to work with NGOs, a process which generally takes much longer. Interestingly enough, most of the professional agencies were aware of these problems, but did not see any other option for coping with these huge resource allocations.

*Strengthening training and capacity building in the South*

Although there has been a lot of training mainly around the 'Do no Harm' approach, much more training, primarily in the form of capacity building, is needed, especially in the South. There is a need to establish training partnerships with local institutions and governments in the South in order to make better use of local knowledge and create a sense of ownership for peace/conflict sensitivity in development and humanitarian work. We need to avoid institutionalizing Northern-only agency and a consultant-driven approach to conflict and peacebuilding.

*Standardization of planning and evaluation guidelines*

A further challenge is to achieve a certain degree of standardization for planning and evaluating development and humanitarian interventions in conflict zones on similar lines to the OECD criteria for the evaluation of development programs. Such evaluations lose their meaning if each donor and organization starts developing their own guidelines. It would be far more beneficial if this standardization process were carried out with researchers, governmental and non-governmental actors from the North, South and East in the context of an international network. The creation of such a network could have the added benefit of also providing an independent institution that could facilitate knowledge-sharing and joint learning needs while not being a donor dependent INGO (International Non-Governmental Organization). A first step toward creating such a network could be the establishment of a web-based joint learning platform to share information and experiences of the practice of linking conflict, peacebuilding and development as well as professionalization in peacebuilding.

*Towards an organizational integration of the 'Peace and Conflict' lens (Mainstreaming)*

As with many development mainstreaming topics, the peace/conflict lens was introduced by many agencies with a tool-based strategy. It is now time to engage in a more holistic mainstreaming approach that involves all dimensions aiming at systematic 'peace and conflict sensitive policy and program management.'

During the early phase of discussions in the aftermath of Rwanda, we witnessed many separate peace and conflict assessments studying the effectiveness of aid interventions in conflict areas. In the beginning this was mainly done in order to get a general understanding of what peace/conflict sensitivity entails. Often these early assessments were not conducted in a participatory way and also came up with negative results as the peace/conflict topic had not been incorporated into aid planning previously. Consequently, these results often spawned negative feelings about the issue among program staff, who are already overwhelmed by all sorts of mainstreaming topics (gender, environment, HIV, poverty to name a few) and are therefore skeptical about embracing yet another topic. These experiences have shown that there is a limit to conducting separate assessments, because they are not part of the standard routine of development cooperation and humanitarian action. Nevertheless, these separate assessments are still conducted and have also been the main methodological entry point and means of learning about the topic. However, there is now an increasing trend of incorporating the peace/conflict lens directly into standard aid planning and evaluations.

When comparing the vital international aid agency expert debate on peace and conflict with the reality of implementing peace/conflict sensitivity on the ground, the picture is fairly different. On the one hand, we can see the success of peace/conflict as a new mainstreaming topic; yet, on the other hand, a critical look into the Post-Tsunami aid in Sri Lanka (see example above) in terms of overall distribution and mode of delivery shows how far away the field is currently from an automatic, systematic peace and conflict sensitive aid policy and operational implementation. In practice, peace and conflict sensitive development and humanitarian action is just at the beginning of implementation – although there are many good pilot programs already in existence and a lot of conceptual discussions and mainstreaming efforts are occurring at headquarters and within specialized conflict/peace expert units within donors and agencies.

In the following chapters we will go into more detail regarding: a) how to apply the 'Aid for Peace' framework as a separate Peace and Conflict Assessment for development and humanitarian policies, programs, and projects (chapter 8), b) how to integrate the framework into standard development planning (chapter 9), as well as development and humanitarian evaluations in conflict zones (chapter 10) and c) how to proceed with organizational mainstreaming of the peace and conflict topic.

# 8 Conducting a Peace and Conflict Assessment

## What is a Peace and Conflict Assessment (PCA)?

The objective of a 'Peace and Conflict Assessment' (PCA) is to improve the design and implementation of a development or humanitarian policy or program/project from a peace and conflict perspective. PCAs are comparable to environmental or gender assessments in development.

This chapter gives an overview of how a PCA is conducted with the help of the 'Aid for Peace' framework; how a good process can be designed and prepared through applying the different parts of the 'Aid for Peace' framework, and how to ensure that the results of the PCA are properly used so that the process can be sustained.

PCA evolved out of the PCIA debate at the end of 1990s (see chapters 1 and 7) and was the starting point for the development of the 'Aid for Peace' approach. Development and humanitarian donors and agencies started applying these types of assessments in order to get a better understanding of the effects of their programs on armed conflict and peacebuilding. Peace and Conflict Assessment as an application form of the 'Aid for Peace' approach is specifically designed for development and humanitarian interventions that have just passed the stage of standard aid planning or are already in the implementation phase.

PCA is an assessment methodology that can be used for assessing the peace and conflict relevance, risks and effects of development or humanitarian projects or programs, a development sector or an entire country program of one or more donors or agencies. Conducting PCAs for entire country programs is a longer process that starts at the strategic decision making level of donors, often at headquarters. Here usually Foreign and Development Departments/Ministries are involved. Such a process takes one to two years and the PCA stands often at the beginning of this process; program and project PCAs follow over time. Development sector and development/humanitarian project PCAs are usually one-time events that take place mainly in the field. The results are then inculcated into the implementation of the respective program/project.

A PCA is conducted with the help of applying the 'Aid for Peace' framework (see chapter 2). This framework consists of four parts (see figure 1) that have to be applied successively to conduct a Peace and Conflict Assessment:

First, we need to analyze the *Peacebuilding Needs* of the respective country or area by analyzing the conflict situation and the peacebuilding process (step 1); anticipating future changes in the conflict dynamics and the peace process (step 2);

identifying the peacebuilding deficiencies, and finally specifying the peacebuilding needs.

Second, we need to analyze whether the overall direction of the planned or already existing policy, program or project corresponds with these identified peacebuilding needs. This is done with the help of the *peacebuilding relevance* assessment.

Third, we want to know existing or possible *conflict risks* for the intervention in question due the situation of armed conflict. This is done with the help of a conflict risk assessment.

Fourth, we want to know the potential *positive and negative effects* (outcome and impact) the respective policy, program or project can or could have on the conflict dynamics and the peacebuilding process. Different methodologies are suitable here depending on the respective policy or program (see chapter 2).

Often a worsening political situation in a development country experiencing increasing violence is the starting point for reflection within the donor/agency community. The discussions are usually centered on shifting from working around conflict to working in and on conflict (see explanation in chapter 7). In Nepal, the issue of armed conflict started to be widely discussed within the development community from 2000 onwards – this was four years after the start of the armed conflict. However, only by then had the armed conflict started to affect development work. In consequence, many donors and agencies commissioned conflict analysis studies and PCAs in order to better understand the conflict situation, the risks for their programs, and the effects development work could have on the conflict and peace situation. As in the Nepali case, when some actors start such a process in a country (see GTZ Nepal country study from 2001), others usually follow. Interestingly enough, this is not the case in all conflict affected countries. For example, in Palestine there has not been wide discussion about the link between aid and conflict despite the fact that development work is substantially hindered due to the conflict situation.

In the text that follows we differentiate between the various levels of PCA, i.e. country program, sector, program/project.

## What is a Successful Peace and Conflict Assessment?

A Peace and Conflict Assessment has been successful when the involved stakeholders can utilize the results and have been enabled to continue the process. We have also developed a checklist for conducting a successful PCA:

• Sufficient awareness created regarding the importance of including a peace and conflict perspective into development and humanitarian work when working in a conflict zone;

- the PCA has presented
  - a clear and comprehensive analysis of the peacebuilding needs in the country and in the districts or region where the policy or program in question is being implemented; this analysis has also considered existing knowledge that is available internationally, locally and from the stakeholders of the intervention in question;
  - the conflict risks for the intervention and come up with suggestions to reduce them;
  - already-identified policy or program activities that are at risk for enhancing armed conflict and has prepared proposals to make these activities peace/conflict sensitive – if possible. It often boils down to answering the 'four **W**s' as we like to name it: **W**hat, **W**here, with **W**hom and in which **W**ay we are working (see chapter 7).
  - existing or new activities that the intervention can focus on in order to contribute to peacebuilding;
- the above identified findings of the PCA are also being inculcated into the implementation and monitoring of the respective policy, program, or project, i.e. are part of the implementation action plan, the results chains, and indicators;
- a member of the team of the assessed intervention (or an external person or institution) is assigned with ongoing peace/conflict monitoring tasks, and
- a plan is being developed to build local capacities for peace and conflict sensitivity in order to make use of local knowledge, reduce the dependence on international experts, and contribute to the further implementation of the peace and conflict perspective in the country.

In the following subchapters we would like to show our readers what needs to be done in order to obtain such a successful PCA.


## The PCA Process

The process for conducting a PCA involves a combination of awareness building events and participatory workshops combined with surveys, interviews, group discussions involving all the relevant stakeholders and owners of the intervention from the very beginning and throughout the process. Some of the studies and/or surveys need to be commissioned prior to a field mission while others will be carried out during the mission. A PCA usually takes place both at headquarters and in the field.

The ideal process is comprised of the following seven steps:

1. Preparing the PCA at headquarters
2. Starting the field mission
3. Awareness building or training

4. Further data collection and analysis in the field
5. Conducting the main PCA workshop
6. De-briefing and evaluation of PCA in the field and at headquarters
7. Reporting

In practice some of the above-listed process steps can be seen as optional building blocks. This mainly concerns the training and awareness building steps as well as the additional data collection in the field. It is also possible that a PCA is only conducted at headquarters or field level only; in this case many of the steps are not needed. In our experience there are three main types of PCA processes: a) PCA processes with field mission and additional data collection in the field, b) processes without additional data collection prior to the main PCA workshop and c) processes conducted at headquarters without field missions.

We will now go through the different PCA process steps and sub-steps included in a PCA process in the ideal case scenario, including a field mission and additional data collection and analysis in the field. We will add the other types of PCA processes as examples throughout the text.

## Step 1: Preparing the PCA at headquarters

*Clarifying why we need a PCA: Defining the mandate*

In practice, someone in an organization or a group of people has decided to commission or conduct a PCA – often without a clear idea of what PCA is all about. Now, it is up to the involved experts (or responsible person within the organization) to help clarify the needs of the organization, i.e. why a donor or implementing agency wants to conduct a PCA. It is necessary to ensure that all understand the meaning of PCA and also know what the commissioning organizations expect from the process. Because of this, peace/conflict experts from specialized units/ departments within organizations or external advisors/consultants that are called in for support need to have a clear understanding of their role as advisors.

A clear mandate is essential for the entire process that follows. Unclear mandates can lead to many tensions between the involved actors, both within headquarters, between headquarters and field, and between agency staff and the assessment team. A properly stated mandate is also key to a successful PCA as a means to ensure that the results will be incorporated into the work on the ground.

It is therefore advisable to allocate sufficient time for this step and also to engage in a lot of communication. We have often seen that this step is mainly done via email communication between headquarters, field offices, and sometimes also involving parts of the assessment team. This is a good procedure, but we also found that it is useful to talk directly over the phone or use field staff present at headquarters to have more in-depth discussions about the PCA objectives, results and best process.

Many misunderstandings often derive from the fact that PCA is a new methodology and the peace and conflict topic as such is not widely known in the field. Consequently, it is essential to clarify whether all involved actors have the same understanding of the terms and processes and to arrive at a jointly agreed-upon mandate.

An essential part of such a clarification process is involving the right stakeholders.

*Involving the right people: Selection of involved stakeholders and mission team*

The idea of commissioning a PCA often originates in specialized units or departments at an organization's headquarters, without sufficient involvement by or participation of people from the geographical units or in the field. In the course of the process, this can lead to difficulties and even tensions which may eventually limit use of the results. It is important to make sure that right from the beginning all the relevant people are involved in one way or another.

*For program and project PCAs* it is important to involve at headquarters not only the specialized units but also the respective country desk and development/humanitarian sector experts from donors and agencies such as health, water, or agriculture units. It is important that the PCA assessor(s) be involved as early as possible. In the field, partners, in addition to the respective program staff, must be involved.

It is very important to always involve the leadership of an organization in the process in one way or another. This is an important sign for the involved staff members of the importance of the process. Whenever we conducted a PCA and it was high on the agenda of the leadership, we saw a much higher rate of implementation of the results and stronger follow-up commitments as compared to situations where the PCA was conducted without sufficient leadership commitment.

*For country program PCAs* that assess the entire country program of one or more donors or agencies, the situation is much more complex. In such cases actors' involvement needs to be clarified from the beginning in a political sensitive way. It is necessary to involve all the relevant political actors, such as representatives from Foreign and Development Departments or Ministries and their respective in-country representations. Moreover, a broad representation of the operational organizations needs to be part of process. When conducting a PCA for a donor country program in Sri Lanka, the respective donor government invited all the governmental and non-governmental agencies and organizations involved in implementing programs in Sri Lanka to a stakeholder meeting in the donor country. In addition, representatives from the Foreign and the Development Cooperation Ministry were present. The objective of the meeting was to inform all organizations about the political background of the PCA and get a broader understanding of their needs and expectations with regard to the topic and the planned PCA. The results of this workshop were incorporated into the TOR for the PCA. For another donor's country program PCA in Nepal, this step happened directly in the field and was followed by such a workshop at headquarters after the field mission. Here also political representatives from the Embassy were present as well as the heads of the respective implementing agencies. For country program PCAs it is crucial that the government of the country in question or respective other national entities are involved.

For country program PCAs the timing is also important as a PCA is only one step within the process of adapting a country program to the situation of armed conflict. Moreover, it is necessary to make a clear distinction between the plan for the entire process and the PCA itself. Attention has to be paid not to overload the TOR for the PCA in question.

*Building the assessment team*

The commissioning organization also has to clarify whether sufficient internal expertise and human resources are available for conducting a PCA. Often external experts are consulted and recruited to facilitate the process or to function as assessors; a PCA process is usually conducted by a team. The selection of the PCA team should be guided by a set of criteria and members should have a variety of skills and knowledge (see hints in chapter 12).

*Taking stock: Clarifying what we already know*

Before we can develop the 'Terms of Reference' properly and start with the actual application process of the 'Aid for Peace' framework (see chapter 2), we first need to clarify what information we already have and what still needs to be obtained. In order to answer this question we first need to be aware of what information is needed for implementing the four parts of the 'Aid for Peace' framework:

For Part 1 of the 'Aid for Peace' framework, the peacebuilding needs analysis we need a) an analysis of the conflict dynamics and the peacebuilding process in the country, with both national and regional or district analysis; b) a needs analysis of the aid sector in question, e.g. water health, education, SME also both national and regional/district focusing on those areas where the intervention takes place or should take place.

For Part 2 of the 'Aid for Peace' framework, the peacebuilding relevance assessment we need a) detailed information about the intervention (policy description, program/project documents, program/project proposal, past evaluations), b) information about other donor/agency's activities in the same sector or region/district. We also want to know which actors do apply peace and conflict sensitive approaches to development.

For Part 3 of the 'Aid for Peace' framework, the conflict risk assessment we need a) a list of existing risks that have been identified by the stakeholders of the intervention and information on measures/actions already taken to reduce these risks; and, b) information about other actors' conflict risk management strategies.

For Part 4 of the 'Aid for Peace' framework, the assessment of the peace/conflict effects of the intervention we need all the above-mentioned information as well as the intervention's action plans, existing results chains and indicators – if already developed.

When designing the PCA process and thus also the TOR, it is important to clarify what kinds of information are already available and how and when to obtain the missing information, e.g. what kinds of surveys/studies or workshops need to be commissioned prior to the field assessment and what kinds of information will be collected during the field mission and in which form (survey, interviews, group discussions, participatory workshops). This will avoid unnecessary replication and also better clarify the aims of the field mission.

*Developing the 'Terms of Reference'*

After all these issues have been clarified the process can be tailored to the needs of the specific PCA and the 'Terms of Reference' (TOR) can be developed. The development of the TORs as a joint exercise is a very important tool for building awareness and trust and for achieving clarification. It directly links the clarification of the mandate for the respective PCA with the results of the following steps (see steps 2-4). It is therefore important for potential assessors or facilitators not to accept unclear or unfeasible TORs. Ideally, they should be involved in the process from the very beginning, and therefore would have a say in the framing of the TOR.

In addition to the team's mandate, the TOR should include a description of the PCA process in the field and the mission schedule. It is important to design this process to be as participatory as possible and include sufficient workshops, briefings and de-briefings with the involved stakeholders. Moreover, in some PCAs we conducted, we held a training workshop at headquarters as part of the PCA in order to use the PCA as an entry point for awareness building within the organization. Clear responsibilities for managing the PCA, including a clear and transparent reporting arrangement, are also important parts of the TOR that can prevent possible problems (see a checklist for TORs in chapter 12).

The costs incurred in conducting a PCA should be clarified and agreed upon. It is necessary to be transparent about the needed as well as the available financial and human resources in order to design a realistic and cost-effective process.

The preparation process for the PCA should be finalized with the approval of the TOR. Often donor organizations ask external experts to conduct a PCA and present them with a ready-made TOR. While this may seem like it saves time, as mentioned earlier, the potential assessor(s) should be part of the stakeholder groups involved in TOR development. Another problem arises because PCA assessors are often not aware of all the relevant preparation steps for a PCA as it is still a relatively new assessment methodology. This limits their role as advisors in the preparation process. There is a lack of people that have sufficient knowledge in both the peace/conflict and aid fields. Many organizations call in experts from the peacebuilding field who, unfortunately, often lack sufficient development/humanitarian expertise. Much more exchange between the fields and investment in training and education is needed to overcome these short comings.

*Awareness building or training*

At this point it is also good to decide whether or not to include awareness building or training events at headquarters depending on the respective know how of the involved actors as well as the stage of peace and conflict mainstreaming of the organization (see chapter 11).

---

**Policy PCA without field mission**

It is true that it is also possible to conduct a PCA of a development intervention without a field mission. In reality this rarely happens as the study of the country context and the joint work with the involved stakeholders in the field is an essential part of a PCA. Nevertheless, there might be situations where it is perfectly justified to conduct a PCA without a field mission. This situation makes sense, for example, when a development or humanitarian policy decision has to be made quickly by political actors. We once conducted a rapid PCA of a donor's country program without going to the field: The situation in a conflict country had worsened drastically and prior to going to an international donor meeting, the donor in question wanted to quickly know, a) how experts judge the actual conflict situation, b) how relevant their program was in the light of such an analysis, and c) what entry points for peacebuilding existed through their engagement. We suggested to the donor that it would make sense to conduct a rapid peacebuilding needs and relevance assessment as a basis for internal discussions. However, we also made clear to them that such an assessment would only be a starting point for a future process and that they needed to be ready to also commit financial and human resources in case entry points for action would be identified. As the time frame for the result was only 10 days, we applied the following process: first, we asked a well-known international expert to write up a short analysis of the situation in the country and asked two different experts (local and international) to comment on the short analysis. We then merged the three analyses, highlighting conflicting views, and presented the results at a small internal workshop with the involved actors from the donor agency. During the workshop the participants jointly identified the general peacebuilding needs in the country based on the analysis and mapped their different activities in the country along with their peacebuilding relevance. As a result of this exercise, the donor had a) the feeling of being much better informed about the situation in the country, b) developed a couple of entry points for peacebuilding to be discussed with the other donors during the meeting to come, and c) started to get commitment for adapting the aid programs to the conflict situation. The donor agreed to develop a detailed plan for implementing this process after the donor meeting.

---

*Figure 4: Policy Peace and Conflict Assessments without Field Mission*

### Step 2: Starting the field phase

*Conducting pre-study and surveys*

The objective of conducting a study and/or surveys prior to the actual PCA field mission is to gather as much information as possible to start the field mission and also to save time and resources. It is advisable to conduct these pre-studies and surveys long before the field mission. The idea is that the results, in the form of a report, are ready shortly before the mission team arrives in the respective country.

It is also important to understand what kinds of people can conduct this type of study. We prefer to commission these studies either to local researchers or experts or to local staff of the respective agency. A combination is also an option. Often agencies do not make a lot of use of local researchers because they believe that they are missing an understanding of the development or humanitarian sector. This is sometimes true, but depending on the terms of reference for such a pre-study, the expertise needed mainly concentrates on good political analysis and peace and conflict know-how. In addition, the survey of other actors' strategies can be easily conducted by an agency staff.

All in all, we had mixed experience in regard to the quality of such studies, regardless of whether they were conducted by international or local experts. However, all PCAs we conducted without having commissioned such a pre-study and survey before the actual field mission demanded much more time for the actual field mission, and interviews and workshops held in the field proved to be less targeted due to the missing knowledge – even in situations where we knew the country situation well.

Obtaining a good-quality pre-study depends on knowing the right people and on providing clear and achievable 'Terms of Reference' for this study.

We always give priority to local experts/researchers, in order to include their rich knowledge in the report and to build local capacities for peace and conflict sensitivity analysis. Often good local assessors/researchers can also later be used as experts for the peace and conflict topic.

The objectives of the field mission are to collect further information, create awareness and ownership of peace and conflict sensitivity in the field, and conduct the actual peace and conflict assessment jointly with the involved stakeholders during the main PCA workshop. This workshop can take place at different times during the field mission. The best timing of the PCA workshop is after a field visit to the program/project area where further information is gathered and analyzed. However, in many PCAs we also conducted the main workshop without further field visits due to the security situation in the area that hindered the field visit or because the pre-study provided sufficient insight.

The field mission usually starts in the capital of the respective country. Assuming we had a good preparation process, the assessment team arrives in the country with a lot of information already. In case the PCA is conducted by a mixed team of experts, this is now the first time when the entire PCA team can meet. Often the international experts (external or from the donor or agency) now meet their local colleagues. A minimum of team building and clarification about the mission is needed at this point; but we have always observed that there is insufficient or no time accommodated for this purpose in mission schedules. It is common that the team's first meeting is with the leadership or the responsible person from the organization. This creates an imbalance in the assessment team from the very beginning as the international experts tend to guide the process. Therefore, it is important that time for a minimum of teambuilding is given. This can be even just a joint meal to get to know each other, followed by the first meeting of the mission team where roles are further clarified, a common understanding of the process is achieved and open questions can be discussed. Part of this discussion is taking stock of the situation: the mission team needs to determine what information is missing in the pre-study or survey and adapt the mission schedule accordingly.

During the first meeting with the organization concerned it is important to get clarification on the PCA process with the involved leadership and responsible actors involved. As the mission team has to date mainly dealt with headquarters or via email with the field, this meeting is an important event to solidify understanding of the organization's needs and challenges. Getting the commitment of the leadership is key to success. In case the leadership is not involved in this first meeting, the mission team should try to organize a meeting as soon as possible and try to commit the leadership to being at least part of the awareness building event, and if possible, to have a role in it.

**Step 3: Awareness building and training**

In all the PCAs we conducted we held an awareness building event or often also a training workshop at the beginning of the field mission. This can last between two hours and a full day. We had good experiences when organizations invited many people from other organizations as well to this event. This is a good opportunity to create awareness for peace and conflict issues in the country, and we have always seen participants involved in very stimulating debates that give a first glimpse into their thinking about peace and conflict.

In many cases we also conducted a three to five day training workshop at the beginning of the field mission with the involved staff of the organization in question. Such a workshop facilitates the incorporation of results at the end of mission, creates awareness and ownership, and builds capacity.

The German Ministry of Development Cooperation through its sector program on crisis prevention and conflict transformation has developed a five day tailor-made training course for field staff and partners comprised out of three days general training on peace and conflict sensitive development, instruments and approaches and two days work on the respective German country, sector programs and projects in question. The BMZ's sector program has also build up a pool of internal and external trainers/advisors that are subcontracted to conduct the workshops.

**Step 4: Further data collection and analysis in the field**

Depending on the particular PCA process, different steps can follow at this stage: Either the main PCA workshop is conducted now (please see further down) or further information needs to be gathered in the capital as well as in the program/project area.

In general, *for country program PCAs* more time is spent in the capital to conduct interviews or group discussions with respective stakeholders including local partners, the government of the country and donors/agencies (see list of people for interviews in chapter 12).

*For program and project PCAs* it is important to collect as much data as possible in the respective program/project area and also to hold meetings or workshops with project/program staff and partners.

The objective of this data collection is to get sufficient information to be able to present to the organization a clear and comprehensive analysis of the peacebuilding needs in the country, districts, or region where the policy or program in question is being implemented. Moreover, those issues, groups of people, or geographic areas that need specific attention due to the conflict/peace situation need to be identified for further studies. Furthermore, the conflict risks for the intervention need to be clear and activities that are at risk for enhancing armed conflict need to be identified as well as existing or new activities that the intervention can focus on in order to contribute to peacebuilding. We also want to know what other actors are doing in the same sector and whether and how they incorporate a peace and conflict perspective into their work.

Much of the above information should already have been provided by the pre-study. The purpose of the area visit is to check these results, get further information in light of the issues raised in the study, gain a better understanding of the program/project area and finalize the peacebuilding needs analysis. The assessor(s) should also look into potential or existing positive and negative effects of the planned or existing intervention. For additional data collection purposes the mission team conducts interviews, group meetings, or workshops with a variety of different actors who are relevant for the respective PCA (please see list of potential interview partners in chapter 12). It is important to talk to a good ratio of (potential) beneficiaries of the program/project.

For a program PCA in the east of Sri Lanka the pre-study had identified two main issues of concern for peace and conflict sensitive development in the area: communities divided by ethnicity, religion and caste, and the lack of integration of internally displaced persons (IDPs) into the local communities. The major recommendation was that all the different groups needed to be integrated into all development activities to reduce potential tensions and armed conflict and to enhance peacebuilding. When the mission team visited the respective area, we confirmed these findings, and found a situation in which each village and organization was dominated by one of the ethnic and religious groups; however, in each village or organization a different group was dominating. This finding had major consequences for peace/conflict sensitive development in the area. A simple involvement of all relevant groups into development activities would risk only supporting dominant groups. Much more detailed analysis was needed for designing peace/conflict sensitive programs.

---

**Data collection under difficult circumstances: The case of a community development program PCA in Nepal**

When doing a PCA of a national community development program in Nepal, the commissioning agency found it difficult to arrange meetings with beneficiaries due to security restrictions and difficult access to the rural areas due to the geographical situation of the country with high mountains and deep valleys. We somehow managed to convince them that we would not be able to do the assessment without a decent number of meetings with local communities. The agency proposed to have workshops in the district capitals with local NGOs working with these remote communities. We actually held these workshops but also managed to visit some remote communities by driving and walking long distances in the mountains and plains. It was worth all the fatigue, because we got a different picture when comparing the results of the NGO workshops with the results of the community meetings. The NGOs presented us with a fairly nice picture of their achievements in the communities and what kind of development work was still possible under the difficult circumstances of armed conflict. The reality on the ground, however, proved to be mixed. We could confirm most of the activities implemented, while only during the community meetings we received information about the positive and negative effects of the program on the local and district level. We were also able to better assess the difficulties facing these communities as a result of being victims sandwiched between the conflict parties. Most of these communities were totally dependent on one or all of the conflict parties, which put serious restrictions on the way in which community development was implemented. We would not have gained this degree of insight merely by remaining in the capital.

---

*Figure 5: Data Collection under Difficult Circumstances*

After the field visit is complete, the mission team needs to analyze all the information provided from the pre-study as well as that gathered in the field. It is important to have sufficient time for this important task. Unfortunately, we often find packed mission schedules that tend to deny time allocated for this task! Regardless of scheduling constraints, this is a key step within the process as only now the main findings of the PCA will be analyzed and the main PCA workshop will need to be prepared.

The results of the data analysis will be presented first to the responsible person within the agency/donor and, if possible, also to the leadership. This is an important step, because it is necessary to have leadership commitment for the entire PCA process. As a means of confidence building the leadership should be aware of the findings prior to the rest of the staff. It is also necessary to discuss how sensitive findings should be presented in the workshop.

**Step 5: Conducting the main PCA workshop**

The objective of the main PCA workshop is to present the findings of the assessment, create ownership, and jointly develop recommendations and an action plan for follow up implementation.

The main PCA workshop generally starts with a presentation of the PCA process and its main findings by the mission team. In fact, the mission team usually already has a set of recommendations in mind; however our advice is to never present recommendations but to let the stakeholders of the intervention develop their own recommendations. In this way ownership for the results can be achieved and also additional knowledge is brought into the process.

The specifics of how to conduct the workshop vary from assessment to assessment. What is important is that at the end an action plan with clear responsibilities is owned by the involved stakeholders. We have had good experiences with presenting the analysis of the peacebuilding needs and then letting the participants add their own analysis.

*The conflict and peace analysis*

The starting point for the workshop is usually the conflict and peace process analysis in case this has not already been the subject of discussions in previous workshops at the beginning of the mission.

When discussing the conflict analysis, it is always important to be sensitive to the cultural context and to the fact that there are varying words for or connotations of the terms *conflict* and *peace*. In some languages there is not even a word for conflict. As a result, we have to be extremely careful when applying Western words and interpretations of conflict in different cultural settings (see methodology for analyzing conflict and peace in Chapter 12, including a gender lens).

*Analyzing the peacebuilding deficiencies and needs*

We found the peacebuilding deficiency analysis the main methodological challenge when doing a development sector or program/project PCA. Here the analysis of the conflict and peace situation has to be merged with the sector needs analysis. Organizations often want to know, which is first, the conflict/peace analysis or the sector analysis; some even ask if the two can be conducted as one.

In practice, the order depends firstly on what kinds of analysis are already available. We experienced that in most cases a macro-level conflict and peace processes analysis is available for a country in conflict, as well as some sort of macro-level sector needs analysis. In this case, the PCA assessor(s) take the two analyses and check for overlapping issues, geographical areas, or groups of people that need specific attention due to the conflict/peace situation and write these points into the TOR for the pre-study for further research.

In the Sri Lankan example special attention needed to go to the issue of just treatment of all groups of the country. In Somalia one of the root causes of conflict is the scarcity of water resources. When doing a PCA of a country program it became obvious that the water sector needed special attention. For example we looked at water users by groups in combination with exploring options for joint water management committees comprising different clans. In many other conflict countries certain geographical areas need more attention because they have been neglected over time and thus have developed the potential for tensions that could lead to armed conflict.

During the workshop we present the two analyses, including the more detailed findings of the pre-study with regard to the program area (for program and project PCAs), and ask participants to merge the two analyses into one peacebuilding needs analysis for the respective sector. Alternatively, we present the already merged analysis and participants discuss and add to it. It is crucial to incorporate the rich knowledge of the people as they need ownership of the analysis and are the ones that live in the country and know the situation best.

*Peacebuilding relevance assessment*

The peacebuilding relevance assessment follows after this step (see Chapter 2). Here, the participants cluster the main activities of their policy, program, or project to the corresponding peacebuilding needs (see relevance scale in Chapter 12). It is necessary that they discuss each activity and find out whether it corresponds to one of the peacebuilding needs; PCA assessor(s) should facilitate and support this process. At the end of this process there are usually a couple of activities remaining that do not correspond to any of the peacebuilding needs. What often happens at this point is that participants try to make these activities look relevant for peacebuilding as well. There are a couple of reasons that explain this tendency. First, participants who are project/program staff fear they could lose their jobs if their interventions are judged to be irrelevant for peacebuilding. Second, people may also be disappointed when their activities are perceived as not adding to peacebuilding. In these cases the facilitator should check the peacebuilding relevance with them again and try to explain why the intervention is not relevant. One can also point to the fact that the intervention might be highly relevant for development but inappropriate in this phase of the conflict.

Stating this distinction often fuels a confrontation between the relative priorities given to the respective peacebuilding and the development relevancies. The commissioning agencies, who are development agencies, point out that their main concern is development and not peacebuilding. How can they handle the dilemma of setting priorities? The outcome depends on the conflict situation and the priorities of the agencies. The best way to gain clarity on this issue is to launch a discussion about priorities and reconciling competing values. The outcome is also influenced by the level and phase of the armed conflict. Often, development programs are designed and implemented as if there were no armed conflict in the country. It is therefore necessary to discuss with the organization whether it is necessary to wind down some activities while increasing others, or to make a strategic decision to drop some activities or to develop tailor-made programs for specific regions of the country. The final decision about what to do rests with the organization, although it is the task of assessors/facilitators to point out the risk of continuing or ending certain activities.

Part of the peacebuilding relevance also involves returning to the survey of other actors' activities and taking them into consideration when assessing the relevance of the agency's own peacebuilding interventions (see chapters 2, 6 and 12).

*Conflict risks assessment*

The next part of the 'Aid for Peace' framework is assessing the conflict risks. Here checklists can be used that focus on questions relating to the security situation, the political and administrative climate, the relationship to partners and stakeholders, and the relationship to the parties in conflict and other intervening actors (see checklist in chapter 12). Ideally this was done prior to the workshop and results can be presented and discussed now. In case this has not already been done, the methodology can be explained and the task assigned to somebody or a rapid risk assessment be done within the workshop. At this stage of the workshop it is important to either discuss what can be done to reduce these risks or to develop an action plan and timetable for this task. The British Department for International Development (DfID) and the German Technical Cooperation (GTZ) have joined hands in conducting conflict risk analysis and monitoring in Nepal. They have founded a joint DfID-GTZ Risk Management Office that provides advice, training and support for the two agencies and their programs in order to enable their development programs to continue to work effectively even in situations of armed conflict.

*Assessing the effects of the intervention on peace and conflict*

The next part of the 'Aid for Peace' framework is assessing the positive and negative effects the policy, program, or project has on the conflict situation and the peace process (see Chapter 2 for overview and Chapter 12 for details). Again, the assessment team should have identified these effects by now and presented them to the participants. At this point it is important to discuss all of these effects and to integrate them into the program implementation plan.

Depending on the particular program, policy, or project being assessed, the best way to proceed with this part of the 'Aid for Peace' framework varies. As there is a lot of confusion about the assessing of effects in general, the main challenge when facilitating this section is to clarify possible misunderstandings right from the beginning. We know by now that a proper assessment of effects is only possible if a monitoring system with results chains and indicators has been established by the intervention from the very beginning, including a base-line study for comparison with the changes achieved by the intervention (see also Chapters 5 and 12). It is often the case that the associated project or policy interventions have not developed these results chains and monitoring indicators as part of their planning.

Moreover, it is necessary to clarify exactly what level and type of effects should be assessed (the effects of the intervention's outcomes on its immediate peace and conflict environment, or the impact of the intervention on the larger peace context of the country?). In case the wider impact should be assessed it is important to know that attributing all changes in the wider peace process to a single intervention is very difficult. It is also the duty of the assessor to clearly explain the limits and possibilities of different methods to the organization and to suggest possible proposals for assessment.

*For a country program* all of effects cannot be discussed in detail during a workshop. What can be discussed, however, are the main potential or existing issues that all activities within the program have to consider. For example, in Sri Lanka, Yemen, the Philippines and Senegal we discussed in which geographically marginalized areas the country program should work in order to reduce potential negative effects of the intervention. In other cases, like in Nepal or Sri Lanka, we discussed which groups of people need to be integrated more strongly into programming in order to avoid supporting only dominant groups.

*For development sector program or project PCAs* the level of discussing effects is more detailed at this point. One way of reducing negative effects on conflict and strengthening or increasing positive effects on peacebuilding is to include the main findings of the peace and conflict assessment into the program implementation plan. This can be done by going through all of the single activities and checking them against the findings. Alternatively, or in addition, peace and conflict effects checklists can be developed that program staff can use throughout the implementation process. For example, in the Somali case, we checked, jointly with the water program team, which activities needed to include more groups or different groups; which water projects needed to be relocated in order to avoid enhancing existing clan conflicts, and how the composition of water management committees could be adjusted in order to create a means of dialogue for peacebuilding between the groups. In the Sri Lanka SME program we did the same thing, however we also transformed the findings into checklists for partner selection. Many agencies use ready-made checklists like the 'Do no Harm' checklists. We believe these lists give very good indicators and are always an excellent starting point for assessing effects; however, in many cases they are not sufficiently targeted towards the specific intervention. We have found that we always profit from using such checklists and that we could enlarge and specify them in light of the PCA assessment and joint discussions in the workshop.

Another even more detailed process at this point is the joint development of results chains with indicators. When doing the latter it is important to understand (see figure 6 below) that there is no need for separate peace and conflict results chains. The idea is to inculcate the peace/conflict perspective into the aid results chains so that they became part of the routine monitoring of the intervention. This can be done by making use of the above described checklists and by integrating them into each results chain by adding the peace and conflict dimension to the activity level of the results chain (see next box).

---

**Working with results chains:** For example, one of the program results chains for a project looked like this prior to the PCA (we added a couple of issues into one results chain for demonstration purposes):

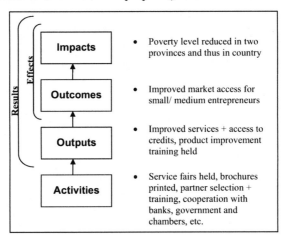

We inculcated the PCA findings in the form of checklists into the results chain by adding issues such as the inclusion of all three languages (Tamil, Singhala, and English) to all training, brochure writing and the peace/conflict sensitive selection of partners along the checklist. When the indicators were developed, how many courses had been held in all three languages and what kinds of partners had been chosen became part of the results chain and therefore the evaluators got an additional indicator.

*In sum, the peace and conflict lens has to be included into the activity level of the results chain and thus automatically becomes part of the entire results chain.*

For all additional activities that had not been planned previously, new results chains need to be developed.

---

*Figure 6: Working with Results Chains*

*Developing a follow up action plan for different scenarios*

After all these steps have been taken, the results and open issues need to be transferred into a follow-up action plan. At this stage of the process it is important to go back to the different possible future developments that were analyzed in Part 1 of the framework (see chapter 2). This is important since recommendations should be developed for different conflict and peace scenarios, because the conditions in conflict situations are subject to rapid change. This is best done by first taking the different scenarios developed in Step 2 of Part 1 of the 'Aid for Peace' framework (see chapter 2) and discussing their likelihood with the stakeholders. The participants then need to discuss the implications of different scenarios for the intervention's activities. It is then necessary to develop implementation strategies for each of the likely scenarios. This is comparable to disaster preparedness planning in humanitarian action.

The participants develop the action plan themselves and directly assign responsibilities. This is the main means to sustain the results of the PCA; it is important to get as much commitment for the follow-up process as possible. All or part of the assessment team can be included in the implementation of the action plan; however, it is important that the role of outsider experts be limited. We recommend relying on local capacities to fulfill these tasks. Often we do not find sufficient capacities for this, in which case it is then worth exploring ways to support building these capacities in cooperation with other actors. For example, the German Ministry of Economic Cooperation and Development through its implementing agency GTZ has supported the establishment of a local poverty impact assessment institution in Sri Lanka over a period of time. The institute is now an important local service provider for research and consultancies in poverty impact assessment. The same could be established for the peace and conflict topic. Another option for smaller projects is to build these local capacities in-house through training of local staff.

Prior to the implementation of the jointly agreed-upon recommendations, it is necessary to make an assessment of the organization's capacity to implement the recommendations. It is not sufficient to just agree on recommendations and assign tasks to the different members of the organization. Often staff are already overworked and will not be able to take care of the implementation of yet another task. It is therefore necessary to assess the capacity of the assigned staff to implement the additional tasks.

When somebody should permanently monitor the inculcation of the conflict/ peace perspective, this often also requires a peace and conflict monitoring system in order to assess changes in the conflict dynamics and the peace process that could effect the intervention's implementation. Organizations need to be clear as to what kind of knowledge is needed to fulfill these tasks. Very often, additional training is required.

In many cases an organization found that establishing such a monitoring system for all of its programs in a specific country is a task that requires additional staff capacities. Many organizations nowadays recruit so-called conflict or peacebuilding advisors or even establish small units to fulfill these tasks for an initial period of two to three years. Others work with short-term consultants to establish the system and train staff to later take over the tasks. Some larger development agencies also establish joint units for different monitoring purposes such as gender, poverty, peace and conflict. In Sri Lanka the donor community has commissioned this monitoring to a Sri Lankan policy research centre that provides three monthly analyses.

**Step 6: De-briefing and evaluation the PCA in the field and at headquarters**

In case not all involved stakeholders have been part of the main PCA workshop, it is important to hold a de-briefing and present the main results of the PCA to these actors at headquarters. We have seen many such situations where the commissioning agency used this de-briefing to invite a greater variety of interested partners and agencies to present and discuss the results with them. This is also a means of further spreading discussion about peace, conflict and development in a given country.

After this de-briefing, the PCA needs to be evaluated. It is best to start the evaluation process with both a self-evaluation and a participatory evaluation before leaving the field. First, a self-evaluation by the assessment team is done which comprises a brief strengths/weaknesses analysis of how the PCA was implemented (how did the team function, how was the relationship between the team and the relevant stakeholders, what were the main constraints) and a brief strengths/weaknesses analysis of the PCA process and its methodologies (What functioned correctly, what did not; where does the methodology need to be adapted). Second, a participatory evaluation is being conducted with the involved stakeholders. This step is best done at the end of the main PCA or the debriefing workshop. A good method is to send participants in small groups and let them do the evaluation by themselves. Third, lessons learned for future PCAs need to be worked out and summarized. The results of the three evaluation steps will be documented for the report. They can be annexed to the report.

After the field mission another de-briefing needs to be conducted at headquarters and the PCA process also needs to be evaluated with the involved stakeholders at headquarters.

**Step 7: Reporting**

After such a PCA process has been conducted, a report usually needs to be written (see reporting checklist in chapter 12). It is important that all relevant stakeholders comment on the report in order to avoid misunderstanding. An indicator of a successful PCA process is when the report writing is more or less reduced to documentation and summary of what has already been discussed and agreed upon among the involved stakeholders.

Another question also emerges at this point: to whom will such a report be disseminated besides the main involved stakeholders? In principle, this should have already been agreed upon in the TOR. In practice, many organizations are not inclined to distribute reports widely. However, it happens regularly that other organizations are very interested in reading the report. This is in fact a good development for spreading the peace and conflict topic. Some organizations therefore make such reports freely available to the public in printed versions and/or on the Internet.

Sometimes it is a good compromise to produce two reports: one for internal use only, including all the details, and one to be published on the Internet for the general public. The latter can be reduced to the analysis of the conflict and peace context and the peacebuilding needs, the general findings and recommendations, a good description of the process and the methodology used.

# 9 Integrating the Peace/Conflict Lens into Standard Development Planning

## Working with Project Cycle Management (PCM) and the logical framework

Project and program planning has a long history in development cooperation and today most organizations have standard planning procedures in place. This is not the case in the peacebuilding field, however, as discussed in Part 2 of this book.

As early as the beginning of the 1980s development project/program planning was improved through the introduction of participatory planning tools, a development that was closely linked to the discussion of participation in development (Cornwall 2002). Participation of the main stakeholders in project/program planning became a means for improving development effectiveness. In the early days of participatory planning, target group oriented planning tools were used that involved the main beneficiaries in the design of the project/program. The most known tool for project/ program planning became the 'logical framework' (logframe), which is a planning matrix that presents a project's intervention logic, assumptions, objectively verifiable indicators (OVIs), and sources for their verification. This framework is usually completed jointly with the stakeholders of the interventions during participatory planning workshops.

Different critiques of the logframe have been aired over the years. The first critique came from researchers from developing countries, who noted that increased participation of people in project/program planning had not increased the participation of people in political decision making in their respective countries (Cooke / Kothari 2001). This critique was partially absorbed into the governance and development debate that started in the beginning of the 1990s .

Another line of criticism posited that poor people in rural areas who are struggling with daily survival do not have time to participate in these endeavors over a sustained period of time. Therefore, relatively 'wealthy' people in the rural areas became the partners in participatory development (Bebbington 2005; Golooba-Mutebi 2004; Putzel 2003). This critique has not really been taken up by the mainstream development discourse.

A third critique was directed against the logical framework as an overly rigid planning tool (see for example the debate of Gasper, Bell and Smith 2000; Dale 2003) that did not consider the complex social and political environments in which projects operate. This view is also supported by many peace organizations that often have a bias against the logframe. They believe that peace issues are too complex to squeeze them into the logframe matrix (see chapter 6). As a consequence of this critique, the 'Project Cycle Management Approach' (PCM) has been developed in the field of development. PCM is a method for the preparation, implementation, and evaluation of projects and programs that combines the logframe with more in-depth analysis of the project/program's general environment as well as sector needs.

Today most development organizations use either PCM or similar methods for program and project planning. Consequently, we have decided to provide a peace/conflict sensitive version of PCM by incorporating our approach into the PCM. This application of the 'Aid for Peace' approach is directed at organizations that are already familiar with planning procedures along the lines of PCM or similar instruments. As a result, we do not go into detail regarding the specifics of planning using the PCM approach (see for example: http://ec.europa.eu/europeaid/qsm/project_en.htm). We have developed a general application that incorporates a peace/conflict lens and it is up to individual agencies to further adapt this model to their specific planning procedures and needs.

## Integrating the peace/conflict lens into PCM

Figure 7 below shows how the 'Aid for Peace' framework can be integrated into the PCM approach for planning development programs and projects in countries affected by armed conflict. As PCM is already a well-developed planning tool, it might astonish some readers that, methodologically speaking, it is not that difficult to integrate a conflict and peace lens into PCM. A well-done PCM already includes a context and stakeholder analysis of the project/program's environment; thus we can build on this already existing analysis by adding an analysis of the conflict situation and peacebuilding. This is best done by integrating Part 1 of the 'Aid for Peace' framework, e.g. the analysis of conflict and the peacebuilding needs, into standard pre-intervention assessments such as the humanitarian or development needs assessment (please see Point 1 in the second columns of figure 7).

After ensuring that such assessment is included in the pre-intervention phase, the main issue we need to watch during the following PCM process and the logical framework exercise is to ensure that the results of this analysis will be included in the upcoming exercise (see points 2-7 in box 2 below). This sounds easy, but it requires a good routine knowledge of both the PCM approach and the peace and conflict lens. The figure below shows how we integrate the peace/conflict lens into PCM by using the 'Aid for Peace' framework:

| Standard PCM + Logical framework | Integrating the peace/conflict lens into PCM + Logical framework |
|---|---|
| 1. Context + Stakeholder Analysis | 1. Integrate conflict and peace context + actor analysis as well as Peacebuilding Needs Analysis *(Part 1 of 'Aid for Peace' framework)* |
| 2. Problem Analysis | 2. Ensure that results of analysis of conflict + the peacebuilding needs are included into the problem analysis |
| 3. Analysis of Objectives | 3. Discuss whether peace/conflict influences the objective or not (this applies for programs with a development or humanitarian goal: e.g. Should 'peace' be integrated as a sub-objective or will it be a cross-cutting issue) |
| 4. Planning with the Logical Framework | 4. Integrate 'Aid for Peace' into Logical Framework |
| 4.1 Formulating the Objectives | 4.1 Deciding whether to integrate peace as an additional objective or sub-objective (*see 3*) |
| 4.2 Formulating the Purpose, Results and Activities | 4.2 Checking purpose, results + activities for their conflict/peace sensitivity (Part 1+2 of the 'Aid for Peace' framework) |
| 4.3 Developing Monitoring Indicators (OVIs) + Source of Verification | 4.3 Integrating the peace/conflict lens into the OVIs (Part 4 of 'Aid for Peace' framework) |
| 4.4 Analyzing Assumptions + Risks | 4.4 Identifying conflict risks and integrating as many as possible into project activities under 4.2 on the left side (Part 3 of the 'Aid for Peace' framework, see challenges below) |
| 5. Activity Plan | 5. Guarantee integration of peace/conflict lens into action plan + staff/experts |
| 6. Monitoring + Evaluation | 6. Monitoring + Evaluation • Monitor OVIs (which should already be peace/conflict sensitive) • Integrate conflict / peace lens into mid-term review + evaluations (*see next chapter*) |
| 7. Budget | 7. Assess + integrate possible budgetary consequences |

*Figure 7: Integrating the 'Aid for Peace' Framework into Project Cycle Management*

# Challenges

Often organizations do not apply the PCM method properly. They do not conduct an analysis of the project's environment but start immediately with the logframe exercise. Thus it is difficult to integrate peace/conflict here. One option for dealing with this problem is conducting a rapid conflict and peacebuilding needs appraisal prior to or during the participatory planning workshop. Another option is conducting a separate conflict and peace analysis prior to the logframe exercise and then use those results.

PCM planning workshops have become routine for development staff. There is, as a result, a high risk that the conflict and peace lens will get lost within this routine, especially during the stages of problem analysis, analysis of program objectives, and the logframe exercise (points 2, 3 and 4 in above figure). The reason for this possibility lies in the logic of the logframe exercise itself: often aid organizations conduct a proper analysis of the project's environment, but when they start with the planning routine, they focus mainly on those needs identified in the sector needs analysis (for example, the needs in the health or water sector). In the process, they forget the rest of the needs identified in the general needs assessment or those related to cross-cutting issues such as conflict/peace or gender. One reason for this oversight is that aid sector experts are involved in the participatory planning exercise. Thus, the only way to forestall this risk is to include a peace/conflict expert in the planning exercise until the conflict/peace lens is more widely known. This inclusion can easily be combined with local capacity building efforts, so that when aid agencies train local institutions to apply the peace/conflict lens they can simultaneously generate a pool of local experts that can support these types of planning workshops.

Armed conflict is seen as a risk factor for projects/programs within the logframe logic; therefore, it does not fit within the activity planning stage, but rather within the risks and assumptions part of the logframe. When this happens, the results of the conflict analysis might be reclassified as risk factors and are thereby omitted from the project activities. Consequently, no monitoring indicators are developed because this is not done for risks but only for activities and results. In response to this problem, we have trained participants in planning workshops to turn risks into activities. For example, during a planning exercise for a water project in a Yemeni district with frequent armed tribal clashes, the participants identified armed conflicts between the different clans as the main risk factor for the project. We reminded the participants that the needs assessment, which included a conflict and peacebuilding needs analysis, concluded that the scarcity of water is one of the root causes of conflict in that district. Thus, any intervention in the water sector risks being involved in the conflict dynamics. The participants then identified a set of project activities to reduce such conflict risks, such as joint discussions with all involved clans about the water project, a water management committee representing all relevant clans, and common leisure activities initiated by the project.

# 10 Integrating the Peace/Conflict Lens into Standard Development and Humanitarian Evaluations

In the beginning of Chapter 5 we gave an overview of the process and purpose of evaluation because it is a relatively new topic within peacebuilding and many peace organizations are not familiar with conducting evaluations. In development and humanitarian work, however, evaluation has been an established component of the program management cycle for decades. Consequently, through years of experience, the development and humanitarian fields have agreed to a set of standard criteria and questions to be used when conducting evaluations.

The subject of evaluations has changed over the years. While in the early years mostly single programs were evaluated, later more evaluations were conducted of entire development sectors or cross-cutting issues. In recent years the subject has shifted again: we now see increasing numbers of evaluations of entire country programs of donor agencies or sometimes even multi-donor efforts in a country. Moreover, the effectiveness of entire governmental donors and agencies is subject to evaluation (Pitman et al. 2005). Along this vein, there are also currently efforts to assess the overall development performance of developing and transitional countries in terms of achievement of results and institutional capacities (Kusek / Rist 2004).

The focus as well as the scope of evaluations has changed over the years. While in the early years, evaluations concentrated on activities and input-output-relations, recently priorities have shifted towards measuring the results of development interventions, e.g. outcomes and impact. To better monitor and assess development impact, results chains and indicators are developed during planning (see figure 6). With the help of these results chains a better link between inputs/outputs and results can be achieved. With the Millennium Development Goals (MDGs) there is a clear set of macro-level policy results with indicators and a set time frame for goal achievement. Because of this, donors and governments of developing countries are asking more frequently about the results of development efforts to reduce poverty, which, in turn, supports the focus on impact.

The ways in which development and humanitarian evaluations are conducted has also been subject to change over the years. At first, most evaluations were conducted by one or more external, mostly western evaluators; it is now standard procedure to involve local as well as external evaluators. Sometimes donors and agency staff are integrated into evaluation teams as well. Contrary to popular assumption, this is not seen as an obstacle to independent judgments, but rather as a useful tool for ensuring the utilization of results and institutional learning. This has also contributed to the application of so-called 'utilization-focused' evaluations (see chapter 5 and Patton 1997). A further development has been the introduction of 'participatory evaluations', which involve all the relevant stakeholders of the intervention into the evaluation process. However, who should be involved and how into the evaluation process also depends on the objective of the evaluation in question (see chapter 5).

Most evaluations in the development field are carried out on the basis of the OECD criteria for evaluations (see, http://www.oecd.org/site/0,2865,en_2157136134047972_1_1_1_1_1,00.html). For humanitarian evaluations, these criteria have been enlarged by the Development Assistance Committee (DAC) of the OECD and 'The Active Learning Network on Accountability and Performance in Humanitarian Affairs' (ALNAP). However, no specific criteria exist for working in zones of armed conflict or in the aftermath of wars or armed conflicts, and the standard criteria have not yet been adapted to these situations. Though the OECD/DAC is in the process of producing guidelines for peacebuilding evaluations, these do probably not include an adaptation of the existing guidelines to situations of armed conflict.

In this chapter we hope to contribute to this debate by showing how the 'Aid for Peace' framework can also be applied to evaluating development and humanitarian interventions in conflict zones. We have checked the above-mentioned evaluation criteria (DAC/OECD and ALNAP) for their validity in terms of conducting evaluations in zones of armed conflict (development and humanitarian). We found out that some of the internationally agreed-upon evaluation criteria can be applied as they are, but most of them need to be adapted to the task of evaluation in conflict zones. As no agreed-upon standard evaluation criteria exist for peacebuilding, we could not borrow from this field. What we did, therefore, was to enrich the standard DAC/OECD and ALNAP criteria for development and humanitarian interventions with results from the debate on 'Peace and Conflict Impact Assessment' (PCIA) (see chapter 7); evaluation concepts used in peacebuilding (chapters 4 and 5); findings in peace research as well as experiences and lessons learned in peacebuilding practice (chapter 4); field testing: we conducted evaluations of development programs in different countries by applying the adapted and new criteria.

As a result, we integrated the peace and conflict lens into the following standard aid evaluation criteria 'relevance,' 'effectiveness,' 'impact,' 'sustainability/connectedness,' 'co-ordination and coherence,' 'coverage,' and 'participation' (see further down).

In the section that follows, we provide practical guidelines for integrating the peace/conflict lens into standard evaluation criteria for use in conflict zones by drawing on standard OECD and ALNAP criteria for evaluating development and humanitarian interventions. After listing each standard criteria and its definition, we describe its meaning for peacebuilding, i.e. its application in conflict zones, followed by an additional set of evaluation questions and methods to apply when evaluating in conflict zones. Finally, we illustrate this process with examples from our field experience (for more information on evaluation process design, please refer to chapter 5).

## 1. Relevance

*DAC/OECD definition*
The extent to which the objectives of the program are consistent with the needs of the country, beneficiaries and the partners and donor policies.

*Peacebuilding relevance*
The extent to which the program is, in addition to the definition above, consistent with the country's peacebuilding needs as defined in the peacebuilding needs assessment (see chapter 2).

*Additional evaluation questions for conflict zones*
– Do the objectives and key activities of the intervention correspond with the observed peacebuilding needs?
– Have the interventions' stakeholders developed or made explicit a clear and compelling vision for peacebuilding?
– Have the interventions' stakeholders further refined or adapted the intervention's objectives in light of this peacebuilding vision?

*Evaluation methods for conflict zones*
– Conflict and peace process analysis, including a gender analysis (see chapter 12)
– Peacebuilding needs assessment
– Relevance assessment calculated using a relevance scale (see chapter 12)

---

**Evaluating the Peacebuilding Relevance of Development Programs in Nepal and Yemen**

We evaluated the peacebuilding relevance of a donor's entire country program in conflict- affected Nepal. Some programs showed a high degree of peacebuilding relevance in addition to their development relevance, while others were relevant for development only. For example, a program designed to support municipalities at first showed no peacebuilding relevance. After looking at the conflict/peace analysis, however, we saw that the program had recently tried to enhance its peacebuilding relevance through including municipalities in conflict-affected areas as a way of compensating for unjust regional distribution of aid resources. The same was true for a nursing school in a conflict-affected district in Northern Yemen: in the beginning of the project, the school selected nurses using assessment criteria for the health sector. However, after analyzing the area's peacebuilding needs and assessing the project's peacebuilding relevance, the project management introduced new selection criteria that reflected the ethnic/ clan variety in the district as a means of enhancing the peacebuilding relevance.

---

*Figure 8: Evaluating the Peacebuilding Relevance of Development Programs in Nepal and Yemen*

## 2. Effectiveness

*DAC/OECD definition*

The extent to which a program and its activities have attained or are expected to attain their objectives.

*Peacebuilding effectiveness*

The extent to which a policy or program has influenced the conflict situation in a positive way (Do no Harm) and the degree to which it has also contributed to peacebuilding in the immediate environment.

*Additional evaluation questions for conflict zones*

– Has the intervention inadvertently contributed to escalating the conflict situation?
– What process of change has the intervention initiated in its immediate peacebuilding environment?

*Evaluation methods for conflict zones*

The following methods can be easily combined or applied in parallel in order to answer the questions above:

– Before/after comparison (ideally with the help of data from a peacebuilding baseline study that could be also integrated into a development or post-conflict needs assessment (see Kievelitz et al. 2004).
– Evaluation of the results achieved by checking peace/conflict sensitive results chains with the appropriate indicators (see chapter 12).
– In case no peace/conflict sensitive results chains and indicators have been developed, checklists, like the 'Do no Harm' checklist (CDA Web), can be used, or else the evaluators can use assumed peace/conflict sensitive results chains or develop their own checklists (see chapters 8 and 12).

---

**Evaluating the Peacebuilding Effectiveness of Water Projects in Angola**

When evaluating the peacebuilding effectiveness of two water rehabilitation programs in post-war Angola, we found totally different results: one agency had planned its program using only development criteria and set up water points at those areas indicated by the water feasibility study. This led to serious tensions between the two villages located in the area. One village was full of returning refugees belonging to the former conflict party UNITA, while most of the inhabitants of the other village belonged to the other former conflict party, the ruling MPLA party. As the new water point was much closer to the 'MPLA' village, the 'UNITA' villagers saw this as proof that the MPLA government was monopolizing aid resources for their supporters and that aid agencies were working hand-in-hand with them.

---

In the second water program the aid agency had conducted a water feasibility study and additionally a participatory conflict/peace analysis: They had invited the conflicting stakeholders to jointly decide where the water points should be established (taking into account both the development feasibility study and the conflict/peace analysis), and also established joint water management committees. Thus, the program did 'no harm' to the conflict situation and also contributed to local peacebuilding through the joint committees. Both of these evaluations faced a couple of challenges: both agencies had not developed any results chains with indicators, so the 'normal' development evaluation turned out to be difficult, combined with the problems of limited access to the program areas due to land mines. In order to compensate for these problems, we worked with assumed results chains and checklists as well as tried to visit all the locations that were accessible, which meant we could not construct a truly representative sample.

*Figure 9: Evaluating the Peacebuilding Effectiveness of Water Projects in Angola*

### 3. Impact

*DAC/OECD definition*

Impact relates to the long-term effects of an intervention.

*Peace/conflict impact:*

Peace and conflict impact relates to the macro-level peace process and explores whether a development or humanitarian intervention has contributed to macro-level peacebuilding in a positive or negative way. We found out that this additional criterion only makes sense for macro-level development policies or program interventions, for example, for a national poverty reduction programs (PRSP) or for comparative macro evaluations of long-term impacts. For example, the UNDP Bureau of Crisis Prevention and Recovery has commissioned an evaluation of all post-conflict interventions that had taken place in countries with a UN mandate to find out the long-term, impact of all interventions on human security of people.

*Additional evaluation questions for conflict zones*

– What kinds of positive and negative changes in the macro-level peacebuilding process have been initiated by the intervention?

*Evaluation methods for conflict zones*

The same methods as were used for evaluating peacebuilding effectiveness can also be applied here; however, the evaluators should take the macro context into account.

## 4. Sustainability/Connectedness

*DAC/OECD or ALNAP definition*

Sustainability assesses whether the benefits of an activity are likely to continue after donor funding has been withdrawn. Connectedness assures that activities of a short-term emergency nature are carried out in a context which takes longer-term and interconnected problems into account.

*Peacebuilding sustainability*

Evaluators should investigate whether an aid intervention has also contributed to the building of sustainable structures that support peacebuilding.

*Additional evaluation questions for conflict zones*

- Which steps have been taken or are planned to create long-term processes, structures and institutions that support peacebuilding in addition to the primary program objective?
- Does planning and implementation empower stakeholders to develop structures that will have the potential to contribute to conflict management and peacebuilding?

*Evaluation methods for conflict zones*

Assessment of changes initiated in institutional structures and processes, including the effectiveness of such changes.

---

**Sustaining Development Work in Conflict Zones**

After the 2002 ceasefire agreement in Sri Lanka, a German funded GTZ emergency education programs in the most conflict-affected districts in Northern Sri Lanka was started to quickly compensate losses in education by the Tamil population. Next to the actual school activities, the program established education committees comprised of representatives from both conflict parties. These committees became an important dialogue forum for the parties, while the official dialogue on the macro-level was blocked. These meetings were sustained even after the end of the program.

---

*Figure 10: Sustaining Development Work in Conflict Zones*

## 5. Coordination and Coherence

*European Commission/ALNAP definition*

Whether actors in the same field are working towards the same goals and whether the interventions are being planned and implemented in a coherent manner.

*Peacebuilding coherence*

Evaluators in conflict zones need to assess whether actors in the same sector/field are working towards the same peacebuilding goals.

*Additional evaluation questions for conflict zones*

– Do the different actors work towards a common goal/strategy?
– What coordinated forums exist for discussing peace/conflict issues?
– Is there coordination among the donors, agencies, and NGOs with regard to conflict and peacebuilding?
– Do actors consider the peace and conflict strategies of other intervening actors during planning and implementation?

*Evaluation methods for conflict zones*

Comparative assessment of different actors' peace/conflict strategies, activities, and structures for cooperation.

---

**Multi-donor Coordination Forums in Different Conflict Countries**

In conflict affected Somalia, donors and NGOs discuss the effects of the conflict on aid as well as joint possibilities for influencing the peace process within different forums of the Somalia Aid Coordination Body. In Nepal, donors have established the Peace Support Group as well as a donor/agency forum where they managed to establish Joint Operating Guidelines for working in conflict-affected areas of the country. In Uganda, donors have also jointly developed principles for donor interventions in conflict prone Northern Uganda. In Sri Lanka the donor working group on the peace process has jointly developed different future scenarios for the conflict and peace process and has commissioned the monitoring of the peace process and the conflict dynamics to a local research institution. The objective is to jointly analyze the results and adapt programs accordingly. The main characteristic of most of these forums is that they are good at information sharing and poor at formulating coherent action. However, long-term peacebuilding and human security seems to be better achieved through a coherent, but not necessarily coordinated strategy as reported by the UNDP/ BCPR evaluation of post conflict countries taking the example from Sierra Leone.

---

*Figure 11: Multi-donor Coordination Forums in Different Conflict Countries*

## 6. Coverage

*ALNAP / OECD definition*

The extent to which a humanitarian program reaches the affected population.

*Peacebuilding coverage*

The extent to which a humanitarian program's outreach also takes into account just selection of target groups and thereby contributes to inter-group fairness and prevents possible conflicts relating to the program's resource allocation.

*Additional evaluation questions for conflict zones*

- Is aid provided in ways that benefits one (some) sub-group(s) more than others?
- Do material goods go to one group more than others?

*Evaluation methods for conflict zones*

Do no Harm check (see http://www.cdainc.com)

---

**Unjust Coverage During the War in Mozambique**

In central Mozambique, access to many war victims was limited due to the armed conflict. Only late in the war were humanitarian agencies able to establish humanitarian corridors to which people could flee. However, war victims in the South were better able to access these corridors, which systematically privileged those regions. More than a decade after the war, this regional imbalance still prevails, although it is not only related to the uneven coverage during the war.

---

*Figure 12: Unjust Coverage During the War in Mozambique*

## 7. Participation

*ALNAP definition (under discussion)*

The extent to which a humanitarian program and its projects include other donors, partners, and beneficiaries in the planning and implementation.

*Peacebuilding Participation*

In addition to the above definition, the evaluation of an aid program needs to assess whether program planning and implementation has considered the conflict situation and also involved a fair (in a peace and conflict sensitive understanding) representation of different groups in the program area, the program partners and staff.

*Additional evaluation questions for conflict zones*

- Does the staff recruitment policy advocate for inclusiveness and inter-group fairness in a peace/conflict sensitive manner?

– Does the agency involve all relevant parties to the conflict in program planning and implementation?

*Evaluation methods for conflict zones*

Do no Harm check (see http://www.cdainc.com).

---

**Conflict (in)Sensitive Agency Staff Recruitment?**

In Nepal and Sri Lanka, many groups in society are underprivileged due their caste, religious, or ethnic affiliations. The dominant groups are often privileged in aid program implementation as well as staff recruitment because of their higher degree of education. Many aid agencies have now noticed that this practice disempowers certain groups. Consequently, many agencies have developed new staff recruitment policies and also take these group differences into account when planning and implementing programs.

---

*Figure 13: Conflict (in)Sensitive Agency Staff Recruitment?*

## Challenges

When conducting evaluations in conflict zones, donors and evaluators also face a couple of challenges.

One major challenge stems from the fact that development policies and programs have not generally taken the peace and conflict lens into account during planning. This has several critical implications for the evaluation process: implementing agencies feel they are being treated unfairly by headquarters, who often commission the evaluation, because they are being judged on something they had not integrated beforehand. This can lead to tensions between headquarters and the field, donor and agencies, agencies and evaluators. Therefore, a participatory evaluation process helps also in such cases (see also evaluation process description in chapter 5).

Moreover, without a proper integration of the peace/conflict lens into planning, peace/conflict sensitive results chains and indicators are not likely to have been developed. Thus, the potential positive and negative effects the intervention could have on peace and conflict have not been anticipated nor have the conflict risks for the intervention been assessed. This poses several methodological challenges for evaluators, who then need to work with assumed results chains and checklists, which can only approximate results.

Information collection in conflict zones is more challenging then in 'normal' development situations (see also chapter 12): Conflict situations often polarize societies and it is very hard to know which information is reliable. Conflict traumatizes people, which means that many find it difficult to talk about their wartime experiences. Moreover, in conflict zones access to major stakeholders is often difficult due to security problems.

The consequence should not be to not go to the field, as field visit and contact to the involved stakeholders is essential for evaluations. On the contrary, everything possible should be done, to arrange field visits. However, it is important to be aware of the above mentions possible limitations, select interview partners accordingly, work in a sensitive way (see hints for information gathering in chapter 12) and be flexible in setting agendas and timetables. It is also essential that the commissioning donors or agencies ensure the security of the evaluators.

Moreover, lack of adequate personnel to carry out the evaluation often poses a major obstacle given that few development evaluators have substantive knowledge of peace and conflict issues and most peacebuilding experts lack sound evaluation and development/humanitarian knowledge. Much more capacity building is needed to fill this gap, in developing countries but also back at headquarters. The formation of mixed evaluation teams – comprised of development/humanitarian and peacebuilding experts – can contribute to cross-learning in the two fields (see checklist for knowledge and skills in chapter 12). When the mixed teams include both local and external evaluators the potential for knowledge sharing is even greater.

Besides all these challenges we believe that evaluation in conflict zones is possible and can profit from the incorporation of the 'Aid for Peace' framework and other tools into standard evaluation criteria, questions, methods and tools.

# 11   Integrating the Peace/Conflict Lens into Organizational Structures (Mainstreaming)

## What is peace and conflict mainstreaming?

'Peace and conflict' mainstreaming is the systematic integration of the peace and conflict perspective as a cross-cutting theme into the organizational structures and procedures of development (and to a lesser extent also humanitarian) donors and agencies at headquarters and in the field.

The objective of this chapter is to give an overview of mainstreaming the peace and conflict perspective into development organizations. The chapter discusses challenges related to this new mainstreaming topic; gives a short history of peace and conflict mainstreaming; describes phases of the peace and conflict mainstreaming process, and presents lessons learned from different peace and conflict mainstreaming processes that we have supported over the last couple of years. The issue of organizational peace and conflict mainstreaming is not directly linked to the methodology of the 'Aid for Peace' approach; however, when applying such methodologies we often find ourselves part of a wider mainstreaming process.

The peace and conflict perspective has successfully entered the official mainstreaming agenda of international donors and agencies. Next to topics such as gender, environment, governance or HIV/AIDS we find 'peace and conflict' on the list of the most important cross-cutting themes to be considered by these organizations. This is reflected in official policy documents, operational guidelines, and organizational structures to support these mainstreaming processes.

However, taking a look at the number of cross-cutting themes or mainstreaming topics on the agenda of development actors, it is not astonishing that donor and agency staff feel overwhelmed by the many cross-cutting themes they should incorporate into their routine program work. This has often contributed to their resistance to taking on board yet another mainstreaming topic.

We find a set of opportunities and problems when assessing the work of specialized units or advisors within donors and agencies dealing with different mainstreaming topics. On the one hand, the installation of these units or posts is key for systematically mainstreaming a topic. Without additional staff capacity, the respective knowledge and support for incorporating a new theme into both the strategic as well as the operational policies and procedures of an organization is not a given.

On the other hand, however, these units or advisors often work separately from the geographical program units that are engaged with the routine development work, or else advisors have been only assigned a small amount of work percentage for mainstreaming purposes.

Moreover, different thematic units and advisors tend to take the same approach to mainstreaming: they start with developing a policy document, produce guidelines for implementation often accompanied by training and a tool box for practical use that is usually generated with the help of pilot applications. In general, this is not a wrong approach for a single cross-cutting theme, however it leaves staff at headquarters and in the field with a set of many tool-boxes without knowing the priorities for application and also often without sufficient staff capacity and know how to implement them.

---

**Models for Addressing Challenges of Organizational Mainstreaming**

The Swedish SIDA, the German GTZ, and the Swiss SDC can serve as models for dealing with different mainstreaming issues. In order to overcome the missing link between the specialized and the geographical units, the SDC is integrating thematic advisors from specialized units with a certain percentage of their work into geographical units. GTZ is moving in a similar direction through its approach of 'strategic thematic leadership.' Different geographical units take the lead for mainstreaming certain cross-cutting issues into their regional work. Extra staff capacity has been added within the geographical units. Training and support is provided by the specialized units. To overcome the problem of multiple parallel mainstreaming processes, SIDA has introduced an information network of the different specialized units dealing with the main SIDA priority mainstreaming topics. The network engages in joint training and strategizing aiming at finding joint solutions to contribute to SIDA's overall poverty reduction framework.

---

*Figure 14: Models for Addressing Challenges of Organizational Mainstreaming*

Moreover, each cross-cutting theme has a different history and different priority for the involved staff. While most people acknowledges the importance of mainstreaming gender and environment into all development activities, this is different with the peace and conflict topic. Not all developing countries have political tension, latent or manifest armed conflicts that put development at risk. Thus, donors and agencies first need to define in which countries, e.g. under which circumstances, the peace and conflict topic needs to be on the mainstreaming agenda.

This has brought the discussion back to early warning (see chapter 7). A variety of donors and agencies have had external or internal early warning systems in place for a couple of years already, but they have been used more for enhancing the organization's general knowledge base regarding working in conflict zones, or at best, for supporting decision- making for country programs in the field. However, these early warning systems have not often been used systematically for decision-making processes at headquarters or to determine 'conflict countries'. Donors and especially Foreign Policy Departments or Ministries, tend to shy away from officially declaring a country a 'conflict country' in order not to threaten their diplomatic relations. Thus, the incorporation of peace and conflict as a mainstreaming topic is left to the voluntary decision of geographical units or regional offices. While voluntary commitment is key to successful mainstreaming, a 'voluntary only' approach risks that peace and conflict are not high enough on the agenda in a country where it might be most needed.

The German Ministry of Development Cooperation's (BMZ) 'Sector Strategy for Crisis Prevention, Conflict transformation and peacebuilding in German Development Cooperation: Strategy for Peacebuilding' has come up with a binding, routine process for incorporating the peace and conflict perspective into development work of all governmental agencies. This includes both, conflict sensitivity as well as the peace added value. The BMZ has taken over the 'Aid for Peace' framework as a methodology to conduct 'Peace and Conflict Assessments' (PCAs) for incorporating the peace and conflict lens into the development work of all German governmental agencies. Such agencies now need to adapt the methodology to their organization's planning, implementation, and evaluation procedures in order to ensure peace and conflict sensitivity when working in a conflict country. Which countries fall in the category of 'conflict countries' is defined by the BMZ once a year with the help of a set of early warning crisis indicators analyzed by the German Institute of Global and Area Studies in Hamburg. The results serve as internal working information and are not published.

## A Short History of Peace and Conflict Mainstreaming

In addition to the discussion that began after the Rwanda crisis, the main trigger for NGOs to start the debate about peace and conflict mainstreaming was the 'Do no Harm' debate that started in 1996 (see chapters 1 and 7). A number of American and European NGOs were part of the 'Local Capacities for Peace Project' and started an organizational mainstreaming process with established focal points for peace and conflict within the organizations. This group trained a pool of trainers for training local partners in the field and at headquarters; partners were also accompanied in focal areas during pilot implementation. This process is still going on (see http://www.cdainc.com).

The main discussion among donor agencies started in 1995 when the Development Assistance Committee of the OECD established an internal discussion process about the link between peace, conflict, and development. Over the years this process was institutionalized within a DAC working group. A number of policy guidelines and tip sheets for operational practice have been published (see http://www.oecd.org/site/0,2865,en_21571361_34047972_1_1_1_ 1_1,00.html) that form the basis for most donor policy papers about conflict, peace and development.

The mounting challenges of post-conflict reconstruction were also a major entry point for peace and conflict mainstreaming. This is especially true for the

Development Banks and UN agencies. The World Bank established its Post-Conflict Reconstruction Fund in 1997 and the UNDP Bureau of Crisis Prevention and Recovery was founded in the same year (see http://www.undp.org/bcpr and http://www.worldbank.org/conflict).

The peace and conflict mainstreaming debate was also fostered by the post-September 11 discussion about the role of development in preventing terrorism, which was quickly absorbed into the general peace and conflict mainstreaming debate (GTZ 2004).

The debate about options and limitations of development in fragile countries also supports the peace and conflict mainstreaming debate as many of these countries are both fragile and conflict countries. Mainstreaming the peace and conflict perspective into development work within those countries becomes one of the strategies to cope with fragile states (see chapter 7).

## Phases of Peace and Conflict Mainstreaming

In an ideal case scenario we can identify a sequence of mainstreaming phases. In reality many of these phases take place at the same time:

---

**Seven phases of peace and conflict mainstreaming in organizations**
1. Awareness Building Phase
2. Analysis and Clarification Phase
3. Pilot Testing Phase
4. Policy/Strategy Phase
5. Organizational Phase
6. Implementation Phase
7. Lessons Learned Phase

*Figure 15: Phases of Peace and Conflict Mainstreaming*

*1. Awareness Building Phase*

The mainstreaming process starts with building awareness about the peace and conflict perspective. Different organizations have experienced different events or debates that trigger this awareness. Often it is a worsening conflict situation in an important country of engagement or else the international debate among NGOs or donors (see above) served as a trigger. During this phase, a critical number of people within the organization begin to take the lead in further pursuing the issue.

*2. Analysis and Clarification Phase*

When the peace and conflict topic has gained sufficient momentum within the organization, the organization starts defining why and in which way the peace and conflict topic is important. They ask questions such as:

*Mandate*: Does the peace and conflict topic fit in with our mandate (Lange 2005)?

*Goal*: How is the topic treated within our organization? Are we aiming at establishing a new cross-cutting issue or are we just testing in which direction we should go with the topic? (Lange 2005)

*Expertise*: Do we have sufficient skills and expertise to proceed with the peace and conflict topic?

*Commitment*: Do we have sufficient commitment in our organization to further engage with this topic?

*Responsibility*: Is there somebody in our organization who can take the lead and responsibility for further pursuing the topic?

*Resources*: Are we ready to commit additional resources to engage with the peace and conflict topic?

These questions are often discussed by an internal working group. After such clarification and analysis of capacities, skills and responsibilities, the pilot testing phase begins. To define responsibilities already in the early phase of a mainstreaming process is an important success factor: unclear responsibilities can lead to unclear mainstreaming processes.

*3. Pilot Testing Phase*

During this phase the responsible working group, unit or assigned staff start pilot training projects as well as selected implementation to gain experience with the topic. Different organizations have used different approaches to pilot testing:

While many NGOs have piloted through introducing 'Do no Harm' training at headquarters and in the field, many donor agencies have commissioned selected peace and conflict assessment or conflict analysis studies to enhance their understanding of conflict dynamics and peace processes as well as the link between conflict, peace, and their programs. Other agencies have established funds for pilot testing of peace and conflict issues in various developing countries, while again others used a combination of the different approaches.

At the end of this pilot phase often bigger donors and agencies start to assess the results of the pilot testing as a basis for formulating policy or strategy papers.

*4. Policy/Strategy Phase*

During this phase official donor or agency strategies for peace and conflict are formulated on the basis of the international debate, often linked to the core papers of the DAC/OECD working group on peace, conflict, and development (see http://www.oecd.org/site/0, 2865,en_21571361_34047972_1_1_1_ 1_1,00.html) in combination with the results of pilot testing and agency specific issues.

*5. Organizational Phase*

After having received official backing and commitment for further pursuing the issue of peace and conflict within the organization, the main organizational phase begins. During this phase, the essential elements of organizational mainstreaming have to be tackled:

–   Leadership commitment has to be ensured;
–   Further entry points for implementing the peace and conflict lens within the organizations have to be identified;
–   A capacity building strategy has to be developed and implemented;
–   Organizational structures have to be defined that provide support for the process, both at headquarters and in the field, be it a specialized unit in combination with peace and conflict advisors in the field or assigning clear responsibilities for staff in combination with capacity building or starting to build local capacities in the field. No matter what kind of strategy is chosen, without additional staff capacities such a mainstreaming process cannot be implemented;
–   Funds for the process have to be secured: this concerns equally funds for the mainstreaming process itself as well as for implementation. Some agencies choose to allocate a special fund to the specialized unit/staff, others provide 'peace funds' or commit a certain percentage from the country budgets for this purpose.

## 6. Implementation Phase

After all these organizational procedures are set, the routine implementation both at headquarters and in the field begins: Operational Guidelines and procedures have to be developed and implemented according to the needs of the organization. Here the strategic decision of the organization has to be made – in case this is not already fixed within the policy document – regarding whether guidelines are binding or provided on a voluntary basis (see example of the German BMZ above).

The organization also has to decide how to activate the implementation mechanism for applying the guidelines, e.g. who defines when and under which conditions it is necessary to include the peace and conflict lens into the routine development work?

Moreover, support for these processes has to be ensured, which should be part of the implementation of the capacity building strategy. Experience from different mainstreaming processes shows that the capacity that is needed to implement the peace and conflict topic should not be underestimated: An assessment of NGO 'Do no Harm' mainstreaming came to the conclusion that the respective agencies and partners were not able to apply the 'Do no Harm' tool as provided by training without further support and monitoring. Specialized peace and conflict units from donor agencies find it hard to cope with all the requests for support in the field as they have often limited capacities and are short in well-trained, experienced external local and international experts that have a decent knowledge of the peace and conflict topic, development program procedures as well as institutional knowledge that is needed for the specific organizational mainstreaming at headquarters and in the field. Thus capacity building is key.

## 7. Lessons Learned Phase

The lessons learned phase is not the end of peace and conflict mainstreaming, but should be an ongoing accompanying mechanism to constantly incorporate learning.

---

**SDC's Peace and Conflict Lessons Learned project**

The Swiss Agency for Development Cooperation (SDC) runs an applied research project to both document lessons learned and also feed these lessons into ongoing processes within the organization, both at headquarters as well as in the field. The first case study is the Nepal country program. The objective of the project is to
- document how SDC Nepal managed the challenge of armed conflict and adapted the program to the situation;
- to analyze the practice and lessons learned of program management in conflict situations, to draw lessons and derive good practice;
- to feed insights and lessons learned into ongoing processes of SDC's Nepal program;
- to establish a learning team at headquarters with the relevant stakeholders involving the geographical units from the development, humanitarian, political departments, multilateral and the respective thematic units;
- to compare SDC's Nepal experience with SDC's experiences in other conflict-affected countries;
- to feed results and lessons into related SDC processes such as the fragile states working group and other country programs in conflict countries.

The first study on Nepal provides a wealth of findings and recommendations for development work in conflict based on concrete experiences.

Get the study 'Paffenholz, T. (2006): Nepal: Staying engaged in conflict' at http://www.sdc.org.np/

---

*Figure 16: Lessons Learned Project of the Swiss Development Cooperation*


## Lessons Learned From and Success Indicators for Peace and Conflict Mainstreaming Processes

There are a couple of lessons generated from different peace and conflict mainstreaming processes that can serve as success indicators:

*Commitment and Motivation*: From the beginning of a mainstreaming process it is important to ensure commitment and motivation from important persons within the organization. Leadership commitment is essential, both at headquarters and in the field.

*Utilization focus*: The term 'utilization focus' stems from the evaluation field (see beginning of chapter 5). It points to the need that the results of an evaluation should first serve the needs of the involved stakeholders. The same is true for mainstreaming processes. Mainstreaming for the sake of it, does not work – the involved stakeholders must validate the additional dimensions in their development work. An important hint for peace and conflict mainstreamers is therefore to make explicit what is the added value of engaging with the peace and conflict topic. We had good experiences with both pointing to the risks of armed conflicts for development and also providing approaches, methods, and tools that can be easily adapted and integrated into routine work. One instrument for reaching utilization focused mainstreaming processes is participation of all relevant stakeholders.

*Participation and ownership*: It is essential to involve all relevant actors into the mainstreaming process from the very beginning. Specialized as well as geographical units and representatives from the field, including partner organizations, need to be part of the process. Often specialized units have driven the process too much in isolation from the rest of the organization, which results in a lack of ownership for peace and conflict mainstreaming. We have seen more success for mainstreaming when guidelines and tools have been jointly developed with the involved stakeholders instead of presenting yet another set of ready made tools. In the Swiss Development Cooperation Office in Nepal, the Nepali national program officers had been made responsible for the mainstreaming within the Swiss Nepal program.

*Raising awareness and enhancing staff capacity*: A lot of awareness building is also needed on all levels of the organization. Special attention needs to be given to awareness building of the leadership and key geographical units. We had good experiences with providing short informational events for the leadership level in combination with tailor-made practical training courses for the working level of organizations.

*Finding the right entry points:* Where to start the mainstreaming process is an essential component for the success of the entire process. We see two different approaches here: some organizations use a top-down leadership approach to peace and conflict mainstreaming in combination with awareness raising, obligatory procedures, and career incentives related to working in conflict zones in order to attract good people. Actors using this approach often also define in which country the peace and conflict topic needs be considered and how. The other approach taken by many development actors is looking for voluntary entry points in identifying those geographical units or country offices that are interested in applying a peace and conflict sensitive lens to development. We saw the biggest successes in mainstreaming when organizations applied a combination of the two approaches.

*Involving partners in the field*: Another important lesson for mainstreaming the peace and conflict lens is involving the partners in the field at an early stage. NGOs do not have problems with this as implementing projects is often done with local partners on the ground. 'Do no Harm' type mainstreaming particularly targets partner organizations. However, donors and governmental agencies often tend to focus the mainstreaming process on building their own staff's capacity and find it difficult to involve partners. This has often political reasons: the government is the main partner for official development cooperation. However, partner governments are often one party to the conflict (see chapter 7) that is skeptical towards dealing with peace and conflict issues that are highly political. One way of dealing with this problem is a) to involve the working level of governmental organizations into the mainstreaming process or b) to officially keep the mainstreaming process on a development 'technical' level or to engage in parallel political and operational mainstreaming processes.

*Dedicating Resources*: Actors need to be aware of the fact that mainstreaming is not for free and needs additional resources, be it financial or human resources.

*Building strategic alliances and networks*: We saw the building of strategic alliances as another success indicator for peace and conflict mainstreaming. Different alliances are needed here: for donors it is essential to build a strategic alliance with other related Departments or Ministries, such as Foreign Affairs or Defense, in order to reach coherent decisions and prevent blocking each others' political decisions in a country.

The British *Global Conflict Prevention Pool* serves as a model for coherent national strategies. It was set up in 2001 as a new approach to tackling conflict prevention. The purpose of the Pool is to bring together the resources of the Ministry of Defense, Foreign & Commonwealth Office, and the Department for International Development (DfID) to enable a more strategic approach to conflict reduction. It has forged a more holistic view of how to tackle conflict and brought synergy to the Government's conflict prevention work in a wide range of areas such as the Balkans, Afghanistan, the Middle East and North Africa, Nepal and Indonesia.

For NGOs, uniting in a network for cooperation supports the in-house mainstreaming processes. The 'Do no Harm' network is a good example here, where many NGOs join hands for working together. In Germany, the main governmental and non-governmental development and peace organizations and networks have established a joint working group to foster mainstreaming. The Working Group on Development and Peace (FriEnt: www.frient.de) is made up of seven organizations that have different sizes, institutional backgrounds, mandates, and working culture. FriEnt evaluates information about projects and research findings with practical relevance, further develops methodological and conceptual approaches, and promotes the dialogue among member organizations and between members and other institutions. A similar project has existed in Switzerland since 2001 (KOFF: www.swisspeace.org).

*Sustaining the mainstreaming process:* From the very beginning it is important to have clarity about how a mainstreaming process will be sustained. In practice, this means clarifying who is responsible, whether sufficient resources exist for the process, and if there is staff capacity and know-how to support the process. We have seen many cases of well started mainstreaming processes that were spoiled by disregarding these questions. Often organizations make young and inexperienced junior professionals or sometimes even interns responsible for peace and conflict mainstreaming. It is then not the fault of these people that they do not have the necessary expertise to advise and support the implementation of the mainstreaming agenda.

Although knowledge management is a popular issue within development, documentation and lessons learned from different mainstreaming processes are not high on the agenda of development donors and agencies. It seems that often a new mainstreaming topic is started without taking into consideration the rich mainstreaming experiences of other mainstreaming, themes/fields.

In conclusion, mainstreaming the peace and conflict lens into organizational structures and procedures is a complex challenge that needs adequate time, intellectual, financial and human resources, and most of all, commitment and motivation!

# Part IV
# The Devil is in the Details:
# Practical Tools

## 12  Using the 'Aid for Peace' Approach: Answers to Frequently Asked Questions

### What kind of knowledge and skills do facilitators or evaluators need in conflict zones?

- Motivation: real interest and sense of purpose
- Skills needed:
  - Conflict and peace analysis
  - Conflict prognosis or scenario planning
  - Evaluation methods
  - 'Aid for Peace' approach know-how
  - Reporting skills
  - Field experience and a willingness to go to the field
  - Know-how of the intervention type (e.g. development or peacebuilding interventions)
- Attitudes:
  - Trust building, active listening and a willingness to learn
  - Flexibility and creativity; Cultural sensitivity

### How much time does the 'Aid for Peace' process take?

The time needed for applying the 'Aid for Peace' approach depends mainly on its objectives and the type of intervention to be planned or assessed. For example, a process for multi-donor or actor interventions takes more time than a process for a single-donor or single project/program. It is therefore good to first be very clear about the objective and purpose of applying the approach before calculating the necessary time. In the following, you can find some very general ideas as to the time needed for different processes:

Applying the 'Aid for Peace' approach for planning peacebuilding interventions: First, you need to calculate the time for the preparation of the process. Second, you need time for the base-line study. The exact time depends on the intervention's environment. The analysis of the peace and conflict context and the mapping of other actors' interventions can be also included in the base-line study. Third, you need to calculate time for a planning workshop with the stakeholders in the interventions.

Applying the 'Aid for Peace' approach for planning development interventions: First, you need time for the preparation of the process. Second, you can integrate the conflict and peace analysis into the base-line study that will be carried out for the development sector. Third, you need to calculate additional time for the incorporation of the peace and conflict lens within the standard planning workshop. A rough time estimate is two more days when the results of the peace and conflict analysis are already available.

Applying the 'Aid for Peace' approach for assessing or evaluating existing peacebuilding interventions: First, you need time for the preparation of the process. This includes the mapping of other actors' interventions prior to the field trip. Second, you need to calculate time for an assessment, usually done during a field trip. Third, you need to calculate time for a participatory stakeholder workshop. Fourth, you need to calculate a day for a debriefing workshop in the field and at headquarters. Fifth, you need to calculate time for reporting.

Applying the 'Aid for Peace' approach for assessing or evaluating existing aid interventions:

First, you need time for the preparation of the process. Second, you need to calculate additional time for the conflict/peace questions to be assessed, usually done during a field trip.

## What do 'Terms of Reference' look like?

Good Terms of Reference should have the following elements:

- Background: description of the organization's reasons for using the 'Aid for peace' approach
- Objectives and purposes of the specific process.
- Terminology/definitions: this is part of an awareness building process. It clarifies what the 'Aid for Peace' approach is all about and prevents confusion and misunderstandings with regard to terms used.
- Methodology and process: it is crucial that all the different methods and processes that will be used are made transparent. Depending on the particular purpose for applying the 'Aid for Peace' framework, evaluation criteria, methods and tools, PCA steps etc., need to be explained.
- Implementation plan: phases, activities, responsibilities.
- Composition of team: Description of all team members and their functions and tasks.
- Reporting: Description of the reporting procedure, maximum length of report, timing and system of giving comments for the draft report, and when, to whom and in which form (electronically or by mail) the final report should be delivered.
- Time schedule: A precise time schedule needs to be included in the TOR for all activities.
- Management: This is an important but often forgotten element of good TORs. The purpose of this part of the TOR is to provide clarity about who is responsible for what and when.

- Follow-up: The best guarantee of follow-up and organizational commitment is to already suggest ideas for possible follow-up activities.
- Budget: The costs of the entire process need to be listed here.

## What should be considered before going to the field?

You should have the following information and documents before leaving:
- Terms of Reference (TOR).
- Overall information of the organization.
- All relevant policy, program/project documents of the intervention to be planned or assessed.
- All relevant material needed to conduct the 'Aid for Peace' process (material for doing training, conflict analysis tools, etc.).
- All relevant information with regard to the conflict and peace situation in the country.
- Timetable for mission.
- Sufficient information about the country (geography, culture, religion, politics).
- Logistics such as travel schedule; telephone and addresses of hotel, organization, your embassy; transport, visa, money, vaccinations required or climate information.
- Security requirements: ask the organization to provide you with information on security restrictions and their security policy and guidelines.

## What does an assessment team look like?

- *International versus national experts.* External, international experts should be accompanied by insiders from the country/conflict area. It is important that local assessors should not be representatives from only one party to the conflict and that they should also not be too closely linked to the organization that is being assessed. External/international experts should be experts in peacebuilding and evaluations or planning. For sector or program assessments an additional expert in the subject should be added to the team or be provided by the organization.
- *Outsider versus insider organizational experts.* An outsider perspective should be complemented and enriched by an insider organizational perspective. Outside experts are often used as facilitators and assessors. However, the team should include at least one person from the implementing organization, and ideally also one person from the donor agency. In multi-donor or multi-agency processes you will often have representatives of different donors/agencies in the team. Often these representatives come from units that are well acquainted with conflict and peacebuilding methods. However, they are often perceived as having an

organizational bias. The outside expert will therefore have the important role of mediating between the different perspectives. These different donor/agency perspectives do enrich the assessments, although some people believe that this undermines the rules of neutrality. Recent experience, however, has shown that this is not actually the case and that internal organizational perspectives are an asset for the process.

- *Senior versus junior experts*: Since PCA or evaluation in peacebuilding is still a new form of assessment, learning is still needed. The addition of people to the team, such as junior experts and newcomers to the field, will enrich the learning process. However, to avoid misunderstandings, it is necessary to clearly state in the TOR the role of the junior members or newcomers and who will take care of the costs for these persons. We have experienced that organizations are often unwilling to pay the costs of juniors/newcomers, however, they do not object to institutional learning. As a compromise we have often shared the costs for the junior members or added interns or interested agency staff to the team.
- *Gender balance*: The team should be gender balanced.

## What are constraints for teambuilding for short term field missions?

Team building for short-term missions always happens under time constraints. Sufficient time should therefore be calculated for a minimum team building effort. We experienced that this hardly ever happens and we often arrived on the spot and met the other team members together with the head of the implementing agency. It is much better to try to meet the other team members before this first meeting, have an opportunity to exchange experiences, and come to a common understanding of the assessment process prior to the first meeting with the organization in the field. This is both a question of effectiveness within the team and respect vis-à-vis all team members.

## How should one analyze conflict dynamics and peace processes?

### Analyzing conflict

Conflict analysis boils down to analyzing the following issues:

*Conflict setting/environment*: The general environment of the conflict, including history, background, phases of the conflict, past and present dynamics, and the international environment.

*Actors*: The parties – the direct players – and their constituencies are identified and analyzed. In addition to identifying the main parties, one should also pay attention to other actors who could either help the principle parties to reach an agreement or derail the peace process. For each of the parties involved, one should assess their power relations. One popular approach to conflict analysis is the 'conflict mapping' guide originally developed by Paul Wehr (Wehr, 1979). This guide emphasizes five aspects which should be adequately considered in any effective conflict analysis: conflict history, conflict context, conflict actors, conflict issues, conflict dynamics. Very often, in practice, conflict mapping is used to map the actors of the conflict.

*Root causes of conflict*: These are the underlying reasons for the conflict. It is important to distinguish between *root causes* and *escalating factors* (see below). Root causes refer to the underlying fundamental incompatibilities of a conflict. This distinction is relevant for understanding both the sources and the dynamics of a conflict, as well as for coordinating the efforts of management and resolution. The root causes must be addressed and eradicated in order to find long-term and sustainable solutions. For example, in the conflict in Nepal the negotiations failed twice because the opposing parties could not agree on the issue of the constitution (new constitution versus amendment of the old constitution). Thus the constitution became an important issue in the conflict (an escalating factor). However, the root causes of the conflict are to be found at a much deeper level, viz. the social, political and economic injustice and inequalities that lead to the exclusion of major parts of the population from the economic, political and social decision-making process (see example in figure 17 below).

*Escalating factors*: These are the more proximate factors that cause a conflict to escalate. Escalating factors are those issues that intensify the root causes or could have the potential to do so. The escalating factors must be identified and tackled, though an armed conflict can be solved even when some of the escalating factors have not been eradicated. Usually only the combination of root causes and escalating factors can make a conflict escalate into violence. The escalating factors in the Nepal example are the poverty that makes a society more vulnerable to conflict, the high level of state corruption that fuels the mistrust of people in the political system, the high level of political polarization of the Nepali society, the escalation of violence by all warring parties and the international war on terrorism, which supports military solutions to armed conflicts.

*Dividers*: It is also important to identify these issues that are further dividing the conflicting parties. A conflict divider is not necessarily the same as an escalating factor. The concept stems from Mary B. Anderson's 'Do no Harm' approach. In the Nepali case, the different positions of the main conflicting parties relating to the constitution is the main divider (see figure 17 below).

## Analysis of peace processes or peacebuilding potentials

To analyze the peace process, it is necessary to describe the planned and ongoing peacebuilding efforts in different sectors and at different levels: peacebuilding environment, timeline of the peace process, and the main issues and actors. We can analyze the following issues:

*Peacebuilding environment*: The general environment of the peace process or any existing peace efforts is described in terms of history, background, phases and timeline of the peace process, past and present dynamics, and the international environment.

*Actors*: All the main actors, or groups of actors, internal and external to the setting, who have a stake in the peace process at all levels of society should be described. This can also easily be done in a mapping exercise such as for the conflict actors. J.P. Lederach focuses especially on the actors at the top, in the middle and at the grassroots level and suggests corresponding intervention strategies This type of mapping is particularly useful for external interveners, as it brings into focus the internal peace actors and helps to find peacebuilding potential. For easy visualization, J.P. Lederach writes the different peace actors into a pyramid.

*De-escalating factors*: De-escalating factors are those issues that have the potential to contribute to de-escalating the armed conflict or tensions. De-escalating factors are issues, persons, or events which should first arise from within the society in conflict. In many African societies, for example, traditional conflict resolution mechanisms – when still functioning – do often have a potential to contribute to peacebuilding. External mediators or interveners can build on these factors for supporting peace efforts in the country in conflict. However, de-escalating factors can also be external issues or events such as a friendship treaty with a neighboring country.

*Connectors*: It is also important to identify those interests held in common by the conflicting parties (connectors). For example, in the conflict setting in Yemen, common cultural events and the joint religion are connectors between the parties. Like the concept of dividers, the connector concept stems from Mary B. Anderson's 'Do no Harm' approach.

Here is an example from an analysis done in a participatory stakeholder workshop in Nepal. It is just an example that does not go into all the details of the conflict. There are, of course, more than the listed escalating and de-escalating factors. In the example you can see that there are usually only a few root causes while there are significantly more escalating factors. There are also some sample connectors and dividers between the conflicting parties.

| Root causes | Escalating factors | Deescalating factors | Connectors | Dividers |
|---|---|---|---|---|
| Pressure for change 'feudal system' to 'modern system' of governance | Human Right Violations from the security forces and the Maoists | Mounting civil society pressure for democracy + peace | Education | Constitution |
| Exclusion of the majority of the population from decision making | Lack of access to justice | Participation of different groups in the local development | Health | Monarchy |
| Social, political and economic injustice and inequality along cast, ethnicity, religious, regional and gender lines | Political polarization | Strengthened youth | | War on terrorism |
| Political ideology and mobilization | War on terrorism supports militarization | Int. pressure for human rights + democratization | | Corruption |
| | State corruption | Maoists + security forces are often tolerating each other | | External mediation |
| | Mistrust of people in political systems/ politicians | Press reporting about conflict | | Private School Education |
| | Role of the king | | | |
| | Disappointed expectations of people | | | |
| | Public service are not available for local people | | | |
| | Poverty | | | |
| | Divided int. community | | | |

*Figure 17: Conflict and Peace Analysis Nepal*

## How can one integrate a gender lens into the 'Aid for Peace' approach?

The precondition for integrating the gender dimension into the entire process is including the gender dimension into the analysis of the conflict situation and the peace process. This is necessary because both conflict and peace are highly engendered issues: women and men play different social and political roles, have different access to political and economic power, and suffer different consequences of violence and war.

This is of particular importance for peacebuilding as the gender dimensions within peacebuilding have different analytical and political importance and foci than the gender dimension within development. For example, in a rural finance project, a gender lens may analyze categories such as the different roles played by women in farming and financing in the agriculture sector as well as the relevant access of men and women to finance resources. In comparison, a conflict and peace sensitive gender lens shows us how war affects men and women differently, what roles they take up within war and peacebuilding, and how the unequal access to decision-making in peace processes and peace negotiations is played out.

In practice this is being done through:

- Integration of a conflict and peace sensitive gender perspective into stakeholder analysis. (The resulting integration will vary, depending on the analysis methodology chosen. For example, within actor mapping, the different roles of women and men need to be analyzed.)
- Integration of a conflict and peace sensitive gender perspective into the analysis of issues (for example, when the methodology of analyzing connectors and dividers is used, the role of women and men also needs to be reflected).
- Ensuring that the results of the gender analysis are built into the next part of the framework (mainly into the peacebuilding needs) in order to guarantee that the gender analysis is been carried over into the next parts of the 'Aid for Peace' framework.

## How does one collect and analyze information in conflict zones?

*Where do I get information for the peace and conflict analysis?*

- Ask the commissioning organization for internal and external reports and briefing papers. Usually donors and agencies draw up conflict analysis reports for many countries that are not published, though they are shared with other donors.
- Have a look at research publications and the Internet (see our weblinks in this chapter).
- Get in contact with regional and peace experts, if possible.
- Make a plan for getting the missing information.

*How do I select interview partners?*

Let field staff know well ahead of time what kinds of people you would like to see, interview, work with or consult. Sufficient flexible time should be provided for additional meetings. The people you would like to meet could include:

- Representatives of the conflict parties (including government officials).
- Staff of the commissioning organization.
- Partner organizations, agencies, contractors, etc.
- Other organizations/agencies/donors of the same type.

- Resource persons from civil society, research or others.
- Beneficiaries and other major stakeholders.
- Ordinary citizens (taxi drivers, teachers, staff of hotel, restaurants).

*How to conduct interviews*

Start developing interview guides to get the information you need in the field. You should prepare an interview guide for each group of persons you will interview. Interview guides are structured questionnaires. After the first interviews in the field, adjustments can be made to optimize the information gathering. Always compare each interview guide/questionnaire with the TOR in order to see whether all aspects are covered.

*How to analyze interviews*

The best tool for analyzing interviews and information gathered is a qualitative content analysis in three steps: Summary, Explication, and Structuration. *Summary*: The collected information needs to be summarized in such a way that you can make use of the content. *Explication*: When doing the summary, you may find out that certain important aspects of the interview were not sufficiently clear. The objective of an explication is to get clarification of these issues. You need to either cross-check the information with other interviews and read additional documents or – if you do not get clarification and it is a very important aspect – ask the interviewee to clarify the issue once again. You can do a short telephone interview or you can ask for another meeting, if really necessary. *Structuration* aims at structuring the summary of the interview in a way that reflects the main issue/lead questions of the process. The easiest way to do this is to use a *reporting form* covering the lead questions of the interview guide for each group of interviewees. During most parts we do not record the interviews on a tape recorder, because conflict and peace related issues are of a sensitive nature and suspicion is high in conflict prone areas. Thus the reporting form becomes even more important since we have to rely on our handwritten notes. Reporting forms are to be used by single assessors, because it forces them to enter the information gathered immediately onto the form and it guarantees that they do not forget major issues. In the event you are part of a team that has split up into different groups, the reporting forms become essential, since in the end one person is usually responsible for drafting the report. She/he must rely on receiving good reporting forms from the other team members.

## Are there any ready made checklists for the Peacebuilding Deficiency Analysis?

We present here two checklists: the first checklist to be used for the macro policy level of peacebuilding and has been development from research findings on conditions for successful peace agreements (see chapters 2 and 4); the second checklist is an example for a sector checklist to be used for the media sectors and has been developed from international standards in the media field (longer lists exists with the author).

| Condition | Description |
|---|---|
| **Ripeness** | The conflict must be "ripe for resolution", meaning that all parties involved in the conflict must have the perception that they can better achieve their goals through negotiation than through fighting. |
| **Different facilitation channels** | Most negotiations fail because there is only one negotiation channel – the official one. There is a need to create different formal and informal channels. |
| **Involvement of all relevant, representative groups** | This is one of the main factors that determine the success or failure of peace agreements. The logic is simple: if not all relevant groups are included in the process, then the ones who are not, will not 'buy into' the agreement, because they lack ownership. To the contrary, they will attempt to spoil the process. Such an agreement will not be representative and cannot be successfully implemented. Not all groups have to sit at the negotiation table, but they do need to be involved in one way or another. |
| **Vision for peace** | During a peace process the different parties to the conflict must develop their own ideas as to what the country should look like when there is sustainable peace. These different visions – or concepts – must be shared and discussed by all relevant sectors of society, whose opinions must then be channeled back to the negotiation table. |
| **Interest of regional powers in peace** | Peace processes do not take place in a vacuum: if the regional powers are not in favor of peace, they may very well become spoilers. Thus it is important to involve them in one way or another in the wider peace process. |
| **International support for the process** | Most peace processes have also failed because of a lack of international support. It is crucial that this support be given in a way that supports the internal peace actors in the country |
| **Quality of a peace agreement** | Lessons learned from different peace agreements show that those agreements are successful that include the following elements: (1) *Good process design*: it is not necessary that all issues be fully resolved within the negotiations. However, it is necessary to install suitable mechanisms, such as forums or regulatory commissions, where these issues can be further discussed. (2) *Power sharing agreements*: it has been demonstrated that elections can be a stabilizing factor for peace only if democratic procedures have already been established in a society Thus power-sharing agreements have proven to be more stabilizing for young peace processes as they create a win-win solution for all actors. (3) *Security guarantees* by regional and international actors are also needed to stabilize the implementation process, in combination with (4) the *financial commitment* of donors to post-conflict peacebuilding. |

*Figure 18: Checklist for Conditions for Sustainable Peace Agreements*

## Example: Media Sector Peacebuilding Deficiency and Needs Assessment

Referring to figure 19 below, for the media sector the 'ideal situation in non-conflict circumstances' is usually not very different from the 'ideal situation in conflict circumstance'. The same principals prevail. However, the conflict circumstances require that certain issues be given more importance, i.e. that they demand special attention or that certain actions need to be taken. The following overview gives some examples of important factors in the media sector, its characteristics under ideal circumstances and its deficiencies in one selected case. Other deficiencies might prevail in different conflict settings. From there it is only one more step to formulating the respective peacebuilding needs. For the sake of greater analytical clarity, this example refers to different levels of analysis, such as the legal situation, the perspective of the media audience and the perspective of the media as a complex organization, where journalists, editors and owners interact. Other important levels not mentioned here are economics and infrastructure, the environment of media institutions, and the perspective of the individual journalist.

| Level of analysis | Ideal Media situation in non-conflict circumstances | Ideal media situation in conflict circumstances | Real media situation: Bosnia | Peaceb. Deficiency – Media sector Bosnia | Peacebuilding Needs media sector Bosnia |
|---|---|---|---|---|---|
| **Audience** | ▲ Access to diversity of media by the population is ensured<br>▲ population has a choice | ▲ Same as in non-conflict situation<br>▲ special attention given to ensuring access to different media | ▲ Access is restricted to media that reflect only the view of one conflict party | ▲ Only access to biased media (especially radio and TV) | ▲ Access to diversity of media, including impartial sources. |
| **Legal environment and legal reality** | ▲ freedom of expression ensured<br>▲ absence of censorship<br>▲ freedom to create media outlets<br>▲ laws are enforced in reality according to law | ▲ same as in non-conflict situation<br>**plus**<br>▲ equal access to gov't information by all media<br>▲ non-discriminatory, non-exclusive media regulations<br>▲ legal reality not spoiled by conflict (media rights, human rights) | ▲ censorship in particular cases due to conflict<br>▲ discriminatory laws and regulations (denial of equal access to information, libel as criminal offence)<br>▲ legal reality: massive violation of media/ journalists' rights, censorship | ▲ censorship by authorities due to conflict<br>▲ discrimination by law<br>▲ violation of media rights, law enforcement contradicts freedom of expression | ▲ censorship needs to be abolished<br>▲ media laws and regulations need to be non-discriminatory and non-exclusive<br>▲ legal reality needs to reflect the existing media law |
| **Media as a social organization** | ▲ relative autonomy for journalists and editors<br>▲ quality guidelines regarding accuracy and impartiality are in place<br>▲ absence of undue interference from owners or politicians<br>▲ absence of self-censorship (journalists cover "taboo" issues and express their own opinions) | The same, plus:<br>▲ balanced, conflict-sensitive composition of editorial staff<br>▲ quality guidelines are strengthened, especially impartiality<br>▲ absence of privileges for one conflict party<br>▲ independence from social pressure by society to take sides | ▲ media outlets forced to take sides<br>▲ negligence of quality guidelines (stereotypes of the enemy)<br>▲ social pressure forces media to violate quality guidelines<br>▲ self-censorship on conflict issues | ▲ media do not fulfill their role of providing comprehensive information<br>▲ quality standards are not met<br>▲ biased reporting on the conflict | ▲ Strengthen media outlets that are providing comprehensive information<br>▲ strengthen awareness of quality standards inside media organization<br>▲ strengthen position of journalists against owners, editors-in-chief<br>▲ ensure freedom from undue influences on media |

*Figure 19: Checklist for the Media Sector Peacebuilding Deficiency and Needs Assessment*

© Christoph Spurk (2004), Institute of Applied Media Studies, Zurich University of Applied Sciences Winterthur/Switzerland (ZHW).

## How does one assess the peacebuilding relevance in detail?

**1. Compare** whether the main activity lines of the planned/existing intervention are responding to the identified peacebuilding needs. To do so, stick the peacebuilding needs (as defined through the Conflict Analysis + Peacebuilding Deficiency Analysis within Part 1 of the 'Aid for Peace' framework with cards on the left side of a pin board. Write the objectives and main activity lines of the intervention on cards in another color and stick these cards in a row next to the cards that are addressing the peacebuilding needs.

### 2. Assessment of Peacebuilding Relevance

*Assessment criteria:*
- An intervention is not relevant for peacebuilding = no activity line responds to any of the peacebuilding needs
- An intervention is highly relevant for peacebuilding = all activity lines respond to all peacebuilding needs
- An intervention is relevant for peacebuilding = the majority of the activity lines respond to the peacebuilding needs
- An intervention has limited relevance for peacebuilding = only very few of the activity lines respond to some of the peacebuilding needs

**3. More detailed analysis** of the peacebuilding relevance of certain activity lines or looking at the priorities of the relevance
- Are the main/most important peacebuilding needs addressed?
- Do the activity lines also respond to the root causes + escalating/de-escalating factors (this is a quality check of your peacebuilding needs assessment)

### 4. Improving the Peacebuilding Relevance
Discuss what could be done to improve the peacebuilding relevance.

# What does a risk assessment checklist look like?

| | Identifica-tion of problems/ risks | Reaction of the intervention towards risk | Concrete (additional) suggestions for coping with problems/ risks |
|---|---|---|---|
| **Security of intervention's location and reach**<br>– Are there security problems?<br>– Is enough security guaranteed for staff?<br>– Is there emergency planning?<br>– What is the relationship with the armed actors?<br>– Can stakeholders in conflict-affected areas be reached? | | | |
| **Political environment**<br>– What kinds of problems and risks is the inter-vention facing due to the political context? | | | |
| **Economic factors**<br>– Is the intervention subject to any economic risks?<br>– How is the economic/resource environment influencing the intervention? | | | |
| **Partners and stakeholders**<br>– Are the partners involved in the conflict set-ting? Could the selected partners pose any risks to the intervention?<br>– Are the selected stakeholders posing any problems to the intervention?<br>– How is the intervening organization perceived by the local people? | | | |
| **Relations with other actors (donors, I/NGO's)**<br>– Are the relations cooperative and/or competi-tive? | | | |
| **Timing of the intervention**<br>– Is the intervention subject to any risks due to its timing? | | | |
| **Other constraints**<br>– Are there other conditions which could hinder the implementation of the intervention? | | | |

*Figure 20: Risk Assessment Checklist*

## What are effects, outcomes, and impacts and how does one assess them?

Outcomes and impacts relate to the *effects* of an intervention on the environment of the intervention. An assessment of these effects is an attempt to differentiate those changes that are attributable to the intervention from changes due to other factors. Thus, an assessment of effects is an attempt to assess what has happened as a result of the intervention. Therefore these effects are often also called *results*.

Outcomes and impacts are two different levels of effects (results). The *outcomes* of an intervention constitute the first level of the intervention's effects. Outcomes refer to the changes an intervention has initiated within its immediate environment. For example, a training project to enhance journalistic skills involves conducting ten training sessions for reporters. The training sessions are the project '*activity*'. The learning of the techniques by the reporters is the 'output'. The fact that the reporters can use these skills to more effectively practice their work is the first level of effects, which is usually referred to as the '*outcome*' of the intervention.

The *impact* of an intervention is the second level of the intervention's effect. It is determined by examining the changes an intervention has initiated within the wider context, which often occur only after a longer time. The fact that the reporters now contribute to more democratic behavior in the country through better and unbiased reporting is a change the project has achieved. To attribute these changes to the project in question is often difficult as there may be many other reasons why there is better democratic behavior in the country. Please refer to figure 6 (see chapter 8), which demonstrates a simple results chain.

We distinguish between different types of effects: *Intended effects* of an intervention are the results that were expected/desired for the intervention from the very beginning (e.g. that the reporters use their skills to contribute to more democratic behavior). *Unintended effects* can have either *positive* or *negative* results. Positive, unintended effects can be, for example, unintended changes that have contributed to peacebuilding (The reporters also contributed to better standards in journalism schools because some of the participants were staff members of these schools, who themselves then initiated change). Negative unintended effects can be, for example, an increase in armed conflict due to the way the reporting was done.

## What is Peace and Conflict Impact Assessment (PCIA)?

Peace and Conflict Impact Assessment (PCIA) for existing interventions is aimed at finding out what kinds of effects (outcomes and impacts) have occurred in the conflict dynamics and the peacebuilding process as a result of the intervention. The term 'Peace and Conflict Impact Assessment' (PCIA) is therefore misleading as in according to the above definition of effects, PCIA investigates both levels of effects: the effects related to the *outcome* the intervention has initiated within its immediate

145

peace and conflict environment, as well as the changes related to the *impact* that the intervention has initiated within the larger peace context of a country. Therefore, some organizations are now using the term 'Peace and Conflict assessment' which is broader.

The peace community does not make any distinction between the two levels of effects on the peace and conflict context. Both are called *'peace and conflict impact,'* although we sometimes also find the term *'peacebuilding effectiveness.'* It is therefore necessary to always be aware of what kinds of effects on the peace and conflict context (immediate or broader) we are talking about and what kinds of terminology we are referring to when discussing PCIA.

PCIA for new interventions is intended to anticipate what kind of effect (outcome and impact) the intervention could possibly produce within the conflict dynamics and the peacebuilding process. At the same time, one wants to develop indicators that will enable the monitoring and measurement of peace and conflict related effects during implementation as well as for use in evaluation.

PCIA is a more difficult task than traditional assessment because conflict and peace are complex socio-political phenomena. Moreover, peace can be the result of a confluence of factors. When, for example, a peace agreement is signed, it is hard to determine which interventions have contributed to achieving the agreement. The assessment of peace and conflict effects can take on different forms in different types of interventions.


## How should one write a report?

A report should have the following elements:

- *Table of Contents*
- *Acknowledgements*: This is the first thing people read. Try to start with some kind words of acknowledgement for the people who supported the process. All persons and groups interviewed need to be thanked, as well as the main people in charge of the commissioning organization who have been responsible for the process both in the field and at the headquarters level. Do not forget to thank people who have provided logistical support.
- *List of Abbreviations*
- *Executive Summary*: should be as short as possible!
- *Introduction and Background*
    - *Background to the policy/program*: as in the Terms of Reference (TOR).
    - *Objectives and purpose* as described in the TOR. If the objectives have changed, this fact needs to be mentioned and justified.
    - *Methodology and process:* You need to make all your implicit and explicit methodology transparent in this chapter.

- *Definition of Terms*: Define all relevant terms (peacebuilding, etc.) that could possibly not be known to the reader.
- *Assessment Team or Facilitators*: Same as in TOR. If there have been changes or persons added to the team, you must list them.
- *Constraints*: It is very important that you list all the constraints that made the envisaged way of implementation of the 'Aid for Peace' process impossible or difficult. Also indicate what kinds of measures were taken to reduce the listed constraints. Sometimes security reasons prevent you from visiting all the envisaged activities or the originally planned timeframe proves unrealistic for conducting a full assessment of all effects. In such case, you need to explain what you did to handle these problems.

- *Findings*: Structure the findings of the report along the criteria to be assessed (in the case of evaluations) or the different parts of the 'Aid for Peace' framework (in case of a Peace and Conflict Assessment).
- *Recommendations*: Present the recommendations in a logical grouping. For example: general recommendations, recommendations for improving the peacebuilding relevance, the conflict-sensitive development aid, the peace added-value of the intervention, and recommendations regarding management and staff requirements, etc. You should have recommendations for all your findings and compare them at the end again with the TOR requirements. You can list all the already agreed-upon follow-up steps (short-term action plan) and add additional suggestions. You can also annex the results of workshops.
- *Evaluation of the process and lessons learned*: Add a short self- and/or group evaluation of the process.
- *Bibliography*: List all the published and internal documents you used.
- *Annex*: Attach all relevant documents, such as: Terms of Reference, mission schedule, important documents of the intervention, list of persons interviewed, workshop minutes, etc.

# Are there any interesting weblinks providing more information?

*Conflict Analysis and Peacebuilding Information*

| | |
|---|---|
| University of Colorado, Conflict Research Consortium: Online Training Program on Intractable Conflict | http://www.colorado.edu/conflict/peace/ |
| International Crisis Group (ICG) | http://www.icg.org |
| Uppsala University: Conflict Database | http://www.pcr.uu.se/database/ |
| Conflict Resolution Info | http://www.crinfo.org/ |
| Beyond Intractability | http://www.beyondintractability.org |
| Arbeitsgemeinschaft Kriegsursachenforschung (AKUF): Hamburg Conflict Database | http://www.akuf.de |
| Swisspeace Foundation | http://www.swisspeace.org |
| University of Maryland: Minorities at Risk Project (MAR) | http://www.cidcm.umd.edu/inscr/mar/ |
| Heidelberg Institute on International Conflict Research (HIIK): Conflict Barometer | http://www.hiik.de/en/index_e.htm |
| Bertelsmann Foundation: Bertelsmann Transformation Index | http://www.bertelsmann-transformation-index.de |
| Swiss Federal Institute of Technology Zurich (ETHZ), Center for Security Studies: International Security Network (ISN) | http://www.isn.ethz.ch/ |
| Conflict Prevention and Post-Conflict Reconstruction Network (CPR) | http://cpr.web.cern.ch/cpr |
| SIPRI: Facts on International Relations and Security Trends (FIRST) | http://first.sipri.org/ |
| Center for the Study of Civil War (CSCW) (Peace Research Institute Norway) (PRIO): Datasets | http://www.prio.no/cscw/datasets |
| Berghof Research Centre for Constructive Conflict Management: Berghof Handbook for Conflict Transformation | http://www.berghof-handbook.net/ |
| Collaborative for Development Action (CDA) | http://www.cdainc.com |
| International Conflict Research (INCORE): Ethnic Conflict Research Digest | http://www.incore.ulst.ac.uk/services/ecrd/ |
| African Centre for the Constructive Resolution of Conflicts (ACCORD) | http://www.accord.org.za |
| Conciliation Resources: Accord Series | http://www.c-r.org/accord/series.shtml |
| Transcend: A peace and development organization for conflict transformation by peaceful means | http://www.transcend.org/ |

*Conflict, peace and development*

| Collaborative for Development Action (CDA) | http://www.cdainc.com |
|---|---|
| Conflict sensitive approaches to development, humanitarian assistance and peace building: Tools for peace and conflict impact assessment | http://www.conflictsensitivity.org/ |
| German Technical Cooperation (GTZ): Crisis Prevention and Conflict Transformation | http://www.gtz.de/en/themen/ uebergreifende-themen/ krisenpraevention/898.htm |
| OECD: DAC Network on Conflict, Peace and Development Co-operation (CPDC) | http://www.oecd.org/department/ 0,2688,en_2649_34567_1_1_1_1_ 1,00.html |
| OECD: DAC Development Effectiveness in Fragile States | http://www.oecd.org/dac/fragilestates |
| United Nations Development Programme (UNDP): Bureau for Crisis Prevention & Recovery (BCPR) | http://www.undp.org/bcpr |
| Interpeace | http://www.interpeace.org |
| World Bank: Conflict Prevention and Reconstruction | http://www.worldbank.org/conflict |
| Clingendael Security and Conflict Programme (CSCP) | http://www.clingendael.nl/cscp/ |
| Conflict, Development and Peace Network (CODEP) | http://www.codep.org.uk |
| Arbeitsgemeinschaft Entwicklungspolitische Friedensarbeit (Gruppe FriEnt) | http://www.frient.de/ |
| Plattform Zivile Konfliktbearbeitung | http://www.konfliktbearbeitung.net/ |
| European Peace Building Liaison Office (EPLO) | http://www.eplo.org/index. php?id=186 |

*Evaluation*

| OECD: DAC Glossary of Key Terms in Evaluation | http://www.oecd.org/ dataoecd/29/21/2754804.pdf |
|---|---|
| OECD: DAC Network on Evaluation | http://www.oecd.org/site/0,2865,en_ 21571361_34047972_1_1_1_1_1,00. html |
| Active Learning Network for Accountability and Performance in Humanitarian Action (ALNAP) | http://www.alnap.org/ |
| Action Evaluation Research Institute | http://www.aepro.org/ |

# List of Acronyms

| | |
|---|---|
| **ALNAP** | Active Learning Network for Accountability and Performance in Humanitarian Action |
| **BMZ** | German Ministry of Economic Cooperation and Development |
| **CDA** | Collaborative for Development Action |
| **CIAS** | Conflict Impact Assessment Systems (see PCIA) |
| **DAC** | Development Assistance Committee of the OECD |
| **DfID** | UK Department for International Development |
| **GTZ** | German Technical Cooperation |
| **ICG** | International Crisis Group |
| **IGAD** | Intergovernmental Agency for Development |
| **ILO** | International Labour Organization |
| **INGOs** | International Non-Governmental Organizations |
| **LPI** | The Life and Peace Institute |
| **Logframe** | Logical Framework |
| **LTTE** | Liberation Tigers of Tamil Eelam |
| **MDGs** | Millennium Development Goals |
| **MPLA** | Movimento Popular de Libertaçao de Angola |
| **NGOs** | Non-Governmental Organizations |
| **PCA** | Peace and Conflict Assessment |
| **PCM** | Project Cycle Management |
| **PCIA** | Peace and Conflict Impact Assessment |
| **OECD** | Organization for Economic Cooperation and Development |
| **OVIs** | Objectively Verifiable Indicators |
| **RPP** | Reflecting on Peace Project by CDA |
| **SDC** | Swiss Development Cooperation |
| **SIDA** | Swedish International Development Cooperation Agency |
| **SME** | Medium Sized Enterprise |
| **TEC** | Tsunami Evaluation Coalition |
| **TOR** | Terms of Reference |
| **UN** | United Nations |
| **UNDP** | United Nations Development Program |
| **UNITA** | Uniao Nacional para e Independencia Total de Angola |

# Bibliography

ALNAP (2002): How to Evaluate Humanitarian Action, Training Handbook, InterWorks/WHO, Geneva.

Anderson, M.B. / Olson, L. (2003): Confronting War: Critical Lessons for Peace Practitioners, Reflecting on Peace Practice Project, Collaborative For Development Action, Cambrigde MA.

Anderson, M.B. (1999): Do no Harm: How Aid can Support Peace – or War, Lynne Rienner Publisher, Boulder Colorado.

Annan, K., A. (2005): In Larger Freedom: Towards Development, Security and Human Rights for All: Report of the Secretary-General. United Nations Publications, New York

Annan, K. A. (2002): Prevention of Armed Conflict: Report of the Secretary-General, United Nations Publications, New York.

Austin, A. / Fischer, M. / Ropers, N. (Eds.) (2004): Transforming Ethnopolitical Conflict, The Berghof Handbook, VS Verlag für Sozialwissenschaften, Wiesbaden.

Avruch, K. (1998): Culture and Conflict Resolution, United States Institute of Peace Press, Washington.

Barash, D.P. / Webel, C.P. (2002): Peace and Conflict Studies, Sage Publications, London.

Bebbington, A. (2005): Donor-NGO Relations and Representations of Livelihood in Nongovernmental Aid Chains, World Development, 33 (6), pp.937-950.

Bell, S. (2000): Logical frameworks, Aristotle and Soft systems. A Note on the Origins, Values and Uses of Logical Frameworks, In Reply to Gasper. Public Administration and Development, 20 (1), pp.29-31.

Belloni, R. (2001): Civil Society and Peacebuilding in Bosnia and Herzegovina, in: Journal of Peace Research, 38 (2), pp.163-80.

Berman, M. R. / Johnson, J. E. (1977): Unofficial Diplomats, New York, NY, Columbia University Press.

Boulding, E. (2001): Designing Future Workshops as a Tool for Conflict Resolution, in:

Boutros-Ghali, B. (1992): An Agenda for Peace, United Nations, New York.

Bush, K. (1998): A Measure of Peace, Peace and Conflict Impact Assessment (PCIA) of Development Projects in Conflict Zones, Working Paper 1, The Peacebuilding and Reconstruction Program Initiative and Evaluation Unit, IDRC Canada.

Bush, K. (2003): Hands-On PCIA: A Handbook for Peace and Conflict Impact Assessment (PCIA), published on the Internet for example under http://www.swisspeace.org/koff/resources_tools.htm.

Bussmann, W. / Kloeti, U. / Knoepfel, P. (1997): Einführung in die Politikevaluation, Helbing & Lichenhan, Frankfurt.

Brown, M. E. / Lynn-Jones, S. M. / Miller, S. E. (1996): Debating the Democratic Peace. Cambridge, MA, MIT Press.

Centre for the Future State (2005): Signposts to More Effective States. Responding to Governance Challenges in Developing Countries, Brighton, Institute of Development Studies.

Church, C. / Rogers, M. (2006): Designing for Results: Integrating Monitoring and Evaluation into Conflict Transformation Programs, Search for Common Ground / Alliance for Peacebuilding / US Institute for Peace, Washington.

Church, C. / Shouldice, J. (2003): The Evaluation of Conflict Resolution Interventions: Part II: Emerging Practise & Theory, INCORE, Londonderry.

Church, C. / Shouldice, J. (2002): The Evaluation of Conflict Resolution Interventions: Framing the State of Play and Emerging Practice and Theory (2003), INCORE, Londonderry.

Cooke, B. / Kothari, U. (2001): Participation. The New Tyranny?, Zed. Books, London.

Cornwall, A. (2002): Beneficiary, Consumer, Citizen: Perspectives on Participation for Poverty Reduction, Stockholm, Sida.

Croker, C. / Hampson, F.O. / Aall, P. (2001): Turbulent Peace. The Challenge of Managing International Conflict, United States Institute of Peace Press, Washington.

Curle, A. (1971): Making Peace, London, Tavisstock Publications.

Dale, R. (2003): The Logical Framework: An Easy Escape, A Straitjacket, or a Useful Planning Tool? Development in Practice, 13 (1), pp.57-70.

Debiel, T. / Terlinden, U. (2005): Promoting Good Governance in Post-Conflict Societies. Discussion Paper, Eschborn, Gesellschaft für Technische Zusammenarbeit.

Doyle, M. W. (1983a): Kant, Liberal Legacies, and Foreign Affairs, Philosophy and Public Affairs, 12 (3), pp.205-235.

Doyle, M. W. (1983b): Kant, Liberal Legacies, and Foreign Affairs: Part 2, Philosophy and Public Affairs, 12 (4), pp.323-353.

Dugan, M.A. (2001): Imagining the Future: A Tool for Conflict Resolution, in Reychler, L. / Paffenholz, T. (2001): Peacebuilding: A Field Guide, pp.365-372.

Eriksson, M. / Wallensteen, P. / Sollenberg, M. (2003): Armed Conflict, 1989-2002, Journal of Peace Research, 40 (5), pp.593-607.

Fast, L. / Neufeld, R. (2005): Envisioning Success: Building Blocks for Strategic and Comprehensive Peacebuilding Impact Evaluation, in: Journal of Peacebuilding and Development, Evaluation Edition, Vol. 2, No.2, pp.24-41.

Fitzduff, M. (2001): First and Second Track Diplomacy in Northern Ireland in: Reychler, L. / Paffenholz, T. (eds.), Peacebuilding: A Field Guide, Lynne Rienner Publishers, Boulder, Colorado, pp. 110-121.

Fitzduff, M. (2002): Beyond Violence. Conflict Resolution Processes in Northern Ireland. New York, NY. Brookings Institute / United Nations University Press.

Fortna, V.P. (2004): Peace Time: Cease-Fire Agreements and the Durability of Peace, Princeton University Press, Princeton.

Galama, A. / von Tongeren, P. (2002): Towards Better Peacebuilding Practice, European Center for Conflict Prevention, Utrecht.

Gasper, D. (2000): Evaluating the ,Logical Framework Approach' towards Learning-Oriented Development Evaluation, Public Administration and Development, 20 (1), pp/17-28.

German Ministry of Economic Cooperation and Development (BMZ), Sector Strategy for Crisis Prevention, Conflict Transformation and Peacebuilding in German Development Cooperation: Strategy for Peacebuilding, BMZ-Konzepte No. 132, Bonn Hune 2005.

German Technical Cooperation Agency (GTZ), Peace and Conflict Assessment: Guidelines (Leitfäden) by Manuela Leonhardt, Eschborn 2007.

German Technical Cooperation Agency (GTZ), Lessons Learnt from the German Anti-Terrorism Package (ATP): Possibilities and limits of Development Cooperation for crisis prevention and peace building in the context of countries at risk from terrorism by Thania Paffenholz and Dunja Brede, Eschborn 2004.

German Technical Cooperation Agency (GTZ), Peace-Building, Crisis Prevention and Conflict Management: Technical Cooperation in the Context of Crises, Conflicts and Disasters by Norbert Ropers, Eschborn 2002.

German Technical Cooperation Agency (GTZ), Crisis Prevention and Conflict Management in Technical Cooperation , Andreas Mehler and Claude Ribaux, Eschbron 2000.

German Technical Cooperation Agency (GTZ), Nepal Country Study on Conflict Transformation and Peace Building by Uwe Kievelitz and Tara Polzer, Schborn 2001.

Golooba-Mutebi, F. (2004): Reassessing Popular Participation in Uganda, Public Administration and Development, 24 (3), pp.289-304.

Goodhand, J. (2006): Aiding Peace?: The Role of NGOs in Armed Conflict, Lynne Rienner Publisher, Boulder.

Goodhand, J. (2001): Violent Conflict, Poverty and Chronic Poverty, Working Paper 6, CPRC University of Manchester.

Hampson, F. O. (1996): Nurturing Peace. Why Peace Settlements Succeed or Fail, Washington, DC, United States Institute of Peace Press.

De la Haye, J. / Denayer, K. (2003): PCIA as a Tool to Move from Conflict-Ignorance to Conflict Sensitivity within Development, Humanitarian Aid and Peacebuilding work, Vol.1, No. 2, pp.49-62.

Ingelstam, M. (2005): Motivation and Qualifications, Katarina Kruhonja interviewed, in: Reychler, Luc / Paffenholz, T. (2001) Peacebuilding: A Field Guide, Lynne Rienner Publishers, Boulder, pp21-27.

Jeong, H.W. (2005): Peacebuilding in Postconflict Societies. Strategy & Process. Lynne Rienner Publishers, Boulder, London

Kaldor, M. (2003): Global Civil Society: An Answer to War, Cambridge, UK: Polity Press.

Kant, I. (1781): Zum ewigen Frieden, Reclam, Stuttgart.

Kievelitz, U. et al. (2004): Practical Guide to Multilateral Needs Assessments in Post-conflict Situations, Social Development Papers, World Bank, Washington.

Kusek, Z.J. / Rist, R.C. (2004): A Handbook for Development Practitioners: Ten Steps to Results-Based Monitoring and Evaluation System, World Bank, Washington.

Lange, M. (2005): Organisational Development for Conflict Sensitivity: The Experience of International NGOs. Journal of Peacebuilding and Development Vol, 2, No.2, 2005, pp.93-98.

Leader, N. / Colenso, P. (2005): Aid Instruments in Fragile States. PRDE Working Paper 5-January 2005, London, Department for International Development.

Lederach, J.P. (2005): The Moral Imagination: The Art and Soul of Building Peace, Oxford University Press, Oxford.

Lederach, J.P. (1997): Building Peace – Sustainable Reconciliation in Divided Societies, US Institute for Peace, Washington.

Leonhardt, M. (2002): Lessons Learned from Conflict Impact Assessment, Journal of Peacebuilding and Development, Vol.1, No.1, pp.39-56.

Linder, W. (1994): Swiss Democracy: Possible Solutions to Conflict in Multicultural Societies, Macmillan, New York.

Miall, H. / Ramsbotham, O. / Woodhouse, T. (1999): Contemporary Conflict Resolution, Cambridge: Polity Press.

Nyheim, D. / Leonhardt, M. / Gaigals, C. (2001): Development in Conflict: A Seven Step Tool Planer, Fewer / International Alert / Saferworld, London.

OECD / Development Assistance Committee (2002): The DAC Principles for the Evaluation of Development Assistance, Glossary of Key Terms in Evaluations and Results-Based Management, Evaluations and Aid Effectiveness, Series No.6, OECD, Paris.

OECD (2001): Helping Prevent Violent Conflict: The DAC Guidelines, OECD, Paris.

OECD (2005a): Principles for Good International Engagement in Fragile States. Learning and Advisory Process on Difficult partnerships (LAP), OECD Paris.

OECD (2005b): Piloting the Principles for Good International Engagement in Fragile States. Fragile States Group (FSG)-Concept Note, OECD Paris.

Orjuela, C. (2004): Civil Society in Civil War. Peace Work and Identity Politics in Sri Lanka, Department of Peace and Development Work, Göteborg

Österle, M. / Bollig, M. (2003): Continuities and Discontinuities of Warfare in Pastoral Societies: Militarization and the Escalation of Violence in East and North East Africa, Entwicklungsethnologie, 12 (1-2), pp.109-143

Paffenholz, T. / Spurk, C. (2006): Civil Society, Civic Engagement and Peacebuilding, The World Bank Social Development Paper No. 100/2006 and Conflict Prevention and Reconstruction Paper 36/2006.

Paffenholz, T. (2006): Nepal: Staying Engaged in Conflict: Experiences and Lessons Learned from Conflict Sensitive Programme Management (CSPM) in Fragile Contexts with Armed Conflict, Swiss Development Cooperation, Asia Brief: Approaches, 14 November, 2006.

Paffenholz, T. (2005a): The Evaluation of Peacebuilding Interventions (Evaluation in der zivilen Friedensföderung), Paper presented at the conference "Evaluation in der zivilen Konfliktbearbeitung", Evangelische Akademie Loccum, 1-3 April 2005, Loccum / Germany; paper to be published in German in "Loccumer Protokolle".

Paffenholz, T. (2005b): Third Generation PCIA, in: Berghof Handbook, Dialogue Series, New Trends in PCIA: http://www.berghof-handbook.net/pcia_newtrends.htm, Berlin.

Paffenholz, T. (2005c): More Field Notes, in: Berghof Handbook, Dialogue Series, New Trends in PCIA: http://www.berghof-handbook.net/pcia_newtrends.htm, Berlin.

Paffenholz, T. (2005d): Peace and Conflict Sensitivity in International Cooperation: An Introductory Overview (2005), International Politics and Society / Zeitschrift für Internationale Politik und Gesellschaft, No.4 2005, pp.63-82.

Paffenholz, T. / Reychler, L. (2005): Towards Better Policy and Programme Work in Conflict Zones: Introducing the "Aid for Peace" Approach, Journal of Peacebuilding and Development, Evaluation Edition, Vol. 2, No.2, 2005.

Paffenholz, T. (2003): Community-Based Bottom-up Peacebuilding, The Life and Peace Institutes Experience in Somalia (1990-2000), LPI Horn of Africa Series, Uppsala.

Paffenholz, T. (2001a): Ansätze ziviler Konfliktbearbeitung, in: Zivile Konfliktbearbeitung. Eine internationale Herausforderung. Schriftenreihe des Österreichischen Studienzentrums – Studien für Europäische Friedenspolitik, Band 8, agenda Verlag, Münster, pp.15-26.

Paffenholz, T. (2001b): Designing Intervention Processes: Conditions and Parameters for Conflict Transformation. In: M. Fischer/ N. Ropers: Berghof Handbook for Conflict Transformation. Berlin: Berghof Research Center for Constructive Conflict Management, Available online at: http://www.berghof-handbook.net.

Paffenholz, T. (2001c): Western Approaches to Mediation, in: Reychler, L. / Paffenholz, T. (eds.), Peacebuilding: A Field Guide, Lynne Rienner Publishers, Boulder, Colorado, pp.75-81.

Paffenholz, T. (2001d): Thirteen Characteristics of Successful Mediation in Mozambique, in Reychler, L. / Paffenholz, T. (eds.), Peacebuilding: A Field Guide, Lynne Rienner Publishers, Boulder, Colorado, pp.121-127.

Paffenholz, T. (1998): Konflikttransformation durch Vermittlung. Theoretische und praktische Erkenntnisse aus dem Friedensprozess in Mosambik (1995-1996). Mainz, Grunewald.

Paris High-Level Forum (2005): Paris Declaration on Aid Effectiveness: Ownership, Harmonisation, Alignment, Results and Mutual Accountability, The World Bank, Washington D.C.

Paris, R. (2004): At War's End: Building Peace After Civil Conflict, Cambridge, Cambridge University Press.

Patton, M.Q. (1997): Utilization Focused Evaluation, Sage Publications London / New Delhi.

Pouligny, B. (2005): Civil Society and Post-Conflict Peacebuilding: Ambiguities of International Programmes Aimed at Building 'New' Societies, in: Security Dialogue, Vol. 36, no.4, pp.495-510, Sage Publications, London.

Putzel, J. (2003): The Politics of Participation. Civil Society, the State and Development Assistance, Crisis States Development Research Centre: London.

Pitman, G. K. et al. (2005): Evaluating Development Effectiveness, World Bank Series on Evaluation and Development, Transaction Publishers, London.

Resource Pack 2004 (Africa Peace Forum, Center for Conflict Resolution, Consortium of Humanitarian Agencies, Forum on Early Warning and Early Response, International Alert and Saferworld) (2004): Conflict-Sensitive Approaches to Development, Humanitarian Assistance and Peacebuilding. A Resource Pack. Available for download at www.conflictsensitivity.org.

Reychler, L. / Paffenholz, T. (2001) Peacebuilding: A Field Guide, Lynne Rienner Publishers, Boulder.

Reychler, L. (2006); Recent Developments in the Research of Sustainable Peace Building Architecture, Cahiers: Center Peace Research and Strategic Studies, University of Leuven.

Reychler, L. & Stellamans, A. (2005a): Researching Peace Building Leadership, Cahiers: Center for Peace Research and Strategic Studies, University of Leuven, 71.

Reychler. L., (2005b): Assessing the Successful Outcome of Peace Negotiations, Cahiers: Center for Peace Research and Strategic Studies, University of Leuven.

Reychler, L. (1999a): Democratic Peace-Building and Conflict Prevention, Leuven University Press, Leuven.

Reychler, L. (1999b): The Conflict Impact Assessment System (CIAS): A Method for Designing and Evaluating Development Policies and Projects, in Peter Cross, Conflict Prevention policy of the European Union, Yearbook 1998/99, Conflict Prevention Network (SWP-CPN), Nomos, Baden-Baden.

Reychler, L. / Musabyimana, T. / Calmeyn, S. (1999c), Le défi de la paix au Burundi: Théorie et Pratique, Editions l'Harmattan, Paris.

Richmond, O. / Care, H. (2005): Subcontracting Peace: NGOs and Peacebuilding in a Dangerous World, Ashgate Publishers.

Rossi, P.H. / Freeman, H.E. / Lipsey, M.W. (1999): Evaluation: A Systematic approach, Sage Thousand Oaks, California.

Rosser, A. (ed.) (2006): Achieving Turnaround in Fragile States. IDS Bulletin 37 (2). Institute of Development Studies, Brighton.

Rothman, J., (2003) Action Evaluation: A Response to Mark Hoffmann's Comments, in: Austin, A., Fischer, M. & Wils, O. (eds.) (2003): Peace and Conflict Impact Assessment – Critical Views on Theory and Practice, Berghof Handbook Dialogue Series, Berlin, pp.83-88.

Rupesinghe, K. / Kuroda, M. (1992): Early Warning and Conflict Resolution, Palgrave Macmillan, Houndmills.

Russett, B. (1990): Controlling the Sword. The Democratic Governance of National Security. Harvard University Press, Cambridge MA.

Schwartz, P. (1991): The Art of the Long View, Doubleday, London.

Senghaas, D. (2005): Frieden als Zivilisierungsprojekt, in: Senghaas, Dieter (2005): Den Frieden denken, Edition Suhrkamp, Frankfurt.

Smith, D. (2003): Towards a Strategic Framework for Peacebuilding: The Synthesis Report of the Joint Utstein Study on Peacebuilding, PRIO, Oslo.

Smith, P. (2000): A Comment on the Limitations of the Logical Framework Method, in reply to Gasper, and to Bell. Public Administration and Development, 20 (5), pp.439-441.

Stedman, S.J. / Rothchild, D. / Cousens, E. (2002): Ending Civil Wars. The Implementation of Peace Agreements. Lynne Rienner Publishers, Boulder Colorado.

Stedman, S. J. (1997): Spoiler Problems in Peace Processes, International Security, 22 (2), pp.5-53.

Tongeren,van P./ Brenk, M./ Hellema, M./ Verhoeven, J. (2005): People Building Peace II. Successful Stories of Civil Society., Lynne Rienner, Boulder.

United Nations (2001): Prevention of Armed Conflict, Report of the Secretary-General on the Work of the Organization, UN, New York.

United Nations (1992): An Agenda for Peace, Preventive Diplomacy, Peacemaking and Peace-Keeping, Report of the Secretary-General pursuant to the statement adopted by the Summit Meeting of the Security Council on 31 January 1992, UN, New York.

Uvin, P. (2002): The Development/Peacebuilding Nexus: A Typology and History of Changing Paradigms, Journal of Peacebuilding and Development, Vol.1, No. 1, pp.5-24.

Uvin, P. (1999): The Influence of Aid in Situations of Violent Conflict: A Synthesis and a Commentary on the Lessons Learned from Case Studies on the Limits and Scope for the Use of Development Assistance Incentives and Disincentives for Influencing Conflict Situations, paper for the Informal Talk Force on Conflict Peace and Development Cooperation, OECD/DAC Paris.

Uvin, P. (1998): Aiding Violence: The Development Enterprise in Rwanda, Kumarian Press, West Hartford, Conneticut.

Wack, P. (1985): Scenarios: Uncharted Waters Ahead, Harvard Business Review, no 5, 1985.

Walter, B. (1997): The Critical Barrier to Civil War Settlement, in: International Organization, 51 (3), pp.335-364.

Wehr, P. (1979): Conflict Regulation. Westview, Boulder & London.

Wood, B. (2001): Development Dimensions of Conflict Prevention and Peace-Building. An independent study prepared for the Emergency Response Division, UNDP. Ottawa: Bernard Woods & Associates Ltd.

Wood, B. (2003): Development Dimensions of Conflict Prevention and Peace-Building. An independent study prepared for the Bureau of Crisis Prevention and Recovery, UNDP: http://www.undp.org/bcpr/ref/undp_pb_study3.pdf.

Woronuik, B. (2001), Mainstreaming a Gender Perspective, in: Reychler, L. / Paffenholz, T. (2001): Peacebuilding: A Field Guide, Lynne Rienner Publishers, Boulder, pp.61-74.

Zartman, W.I. (1989): Ripe for Resolution: Conflict and Intervention in Africa, Oxford University Press, New York.

# ABOUT THE AUTHORS

**Thania Paffenholz** teaches peace and development studies at the Institute of Development Studies, University of Geneva, and has vast field experience in different conflict zones in Africa and Asia. She has been a peacebuilding adviser for the European Commission in the Horn of Africa for four years, has participated in different UN missions, and is currently an advisor to a variety of different governments and agencies, including the UN. She is also a member of the Executive Committee of the International Studies Association's Peace Studies Section. Her recent book publications include *Peacebuilding: A Field Guide* and *Community-Based Bottom-Up Peacebuilding.*

**Luc Reychler** is a professor for international relations and director of the Center for Peace Research and Strategic Studies at the University of Leuven, Belgium. In 2004 he was elected Secretary General of the International Peace Research Association (IPRA). His recent publications include *Democratic peace building, Le défi de la paix au Burundi* and *Peacebuilding: a Field Guide.*